Creating Your
HIGH SCHOOL PORTFOLIO

An Interactive School, Career, and Life Planning Workbook

*From the Editors of
JIST Works, Inc.*

HS 2/01 7.95

Creating Your High School Portfolio

An Interactive School, Career, and Life Planning Workbook
© 1998 by JIST Publishing, Inc.

Published by JIST Works, an imprint of JIST Publishing, Inc.
8902 Otis Avenue
Indianapolis, IN 46216
Phone: 1-800-648-5478 E-mail: editorial@jist.com
World Wide Web Address: http://www.jist.com

Various sections of this printing have been enhanced and corrected from the first printing. You will find some differences in the text and graphics, but the workbook's focus and structure remain the same.

This workbook is part of a curriculum that includes a resume-writing workbook and an instructor's guide. The instructor's guide covers both workbooks. All materials are available separately from JIST.

The three products in this curriculum (including this workbook) are as follows:

- *Creating Your High School Portfolio: An Interactive School, Career, and Life Planning Workbook*

- *Creating Your High School Resume: A Step-by-Step Guide to Preparing an Effective Resume for College and Career*

- *Instructor's Guide for Creating Your High School Portfolio and Creating Your High School Resume*

Cover Design by Michael Nolan

Printed in the United States of America

03 02 01 00   9 8 7 6 5 4 3

Acknowledgment

Based on *Life Work Portfolio* developed by Judith Hoppin and the Career Development Training Institute (CDTI) under a grant from the National Occupational Information Coordinating Committee (NOICC), which also produced the *Portfolio*. Without the work of those authors, advisors, and the NOICC, this book would not have been possible.

We have been careful to provide accurate information throughout this book, but it is possible that errors and omissions have been introduced. Please consider this in making any career plans or other important decisions. Trust your own judgment above all else and in all things.

ISBN 1-56370-517-6

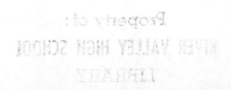

About This Book

A portfolio is a collection of records that will document your education and work history and affirm your successes. This book will show you how to collect and store the documents you'll need when you apply for your first job or for college. It also provides a step-by-step process to help you plan your education and your career path, and it introduces the steps of career planning so that, as you gain experience or your situation changes, you will be able to use this process more than once.

Keep in mind as you are developing your portfolio that you will want to make changes to it as your life changes. Because you are always growing and changing, and because the job market is always changing, you will probably change jobs and/or occupations several times in your life. Your portfolio is the place to keep new information as you change jobs, develop your career, and gain more experience and training. As you learn new skills, you'll document them in your portfolio. As you complete high school, college, or trade school, you'll add your diploma or certificate to your portfolio. When you get a raise, or a promotion, or an award at work or school, you'll indicate it in your portfolio. Your portfolio is an ongoing record of your achievements, skills, experiences, and goals. Your up-to-date portfolio will help you plan your career, and it keeps all the information you'll need for a job search right at your fingertips.

As you research career and education options and set goals, you need to take time to reflect on yourself, your interests, your achievements, and your dreams. It may take a day, a week, or a month to gather together the details of your life, education, and work and arrange them in your portfolio. But it will be a worthwhile investment in your future.

CAUTION

Do not give your portfolio to an employer because it contains personal material.

Table of Contents

Part 3

Part 4

Part 5

Getting and Keeping Your Job 115

Introduction

Most of the topics in *Creating Your High School Portfolio* are followed by worksheets for you to fill in. As you work through the five parts of this book, you should store your working pages (those worksheets you tear out of the book) and other documents in a portfolio for safekeeping.

The portfolio you will create here is a place to store such documents as personal and career planning records; sample resumes; a list of references; a sample, filled-in application; letters of recommendation; special awards and honors; and other job information. You'll also want to keep copies of your diplomas, certificates of mastery, and professional licenses. Your portfolio keeps all the information you will need to make career and life decisions organized and easy to get for review and updating.

Creating Your Portfolio

There are many different ways to make a portfolio; you are limited only by your creativity, time, and budget. Your guidance or career counselor may provide one for you, or you may be asked to provide your own. In that case, you can buy an expensive portfolio system, or you can assemble one very cheaply and easily tailor it to your needs. For instance, you can label file folders with the corresponding parts of this book and place them in an accordion file or expanding wallet. You can also buy pocket portfolios (with or without fasteners) designed to hold papers, or simply label 9" x 12" envelopes for each part. Clear plastic top-loading sheet protectors placed in a tabbed, three-ring binder also hold papers very neatly. You can even color-code the different categories with tabs or labels if you want to. Your portfolio can be as simple or as elaborate as you want it to be. If you have never assembled a portfolio, you may want to start with something simple and make changes to it later as you define your needs.

Your portfolio and the work you put into it will eventually become your own life history. It will help you to look at career options, plan your education or training, write resumes and cover letters, complete job applications, and prepare for job interviews.

Filling Out the Worksheets

Creating Your High School Portfolio follows some basic steps of the career planning process. As you can see below, these steps correspond to each part of the book.

Steps for Career Planning	*Creating Your High School Portfolio*
Looking at yourself	Information on Who I Am
Identifying skills and abilities	What I Can Do
Finding out about career possibilities	Exploring Career Options
Developing action plans	Getting There from Here
	Getting and Keeping Your Job

Planning your life's work will help you make education and career decisions that you'll benefit from for a lifetime.

You'll complete the worksheets in this book by filling in answers or responding to questions. Add more pages as you need them. You should use a pencil or erasable pen so you can change your answers as you gain more experience, learn new skills, and make new goals. Your replies should be just as long or as short as you see fit. Your answers don't even have to be written: you can draw a picture or diagram, record an audio tape of your thoughts, or include the words to a song that has meaning for you. You can take photographs or pictures from newspapers or magazines. Do what makes sense to you as you think about your life, your schooling, work, and goals.

At the end of each section, you'll find a checklist of concepts and skills you'll need for planning your career. Experts in career development say that these are the things a person should know or be able to do when planning a career or job change. You may want to check off the items you understand or the things you are able to do when you finish each section. You'll also find a list of resources to help you explore the basic steps of career planning.

If You Need Help

If you get stuck or decide you need help with your career planning, your school counselor can walk you through the process and help you resolve problems. You may also want to talk your plans over with your parents, your friends, or a mentor—someone who currently does the kind of work you think you'd like to do. The resources listed throughout this book may also be helpful to you. They are available at your local library. There are others in your community who may be helpful to you: career counselors, job trainers, and other professionals who work in a variety of places. Some of these places include the following:

- ▼ Community and government agencies
- ▼ Libraries
- ▼ Adult education programs
- ▼ Colleges and universities

- ▼ Private businesses
- ▼ The military
- ▼ Outplacement firms
- ▼ Corporations

The professionals in these places can help you do the following:

- ▼ Test your occupational interests
- ▼ Match your skills to job possibilities
- ▼ Get more help

- ▼ Write resumes and prepare for interviews
- ▼ Find out about jobs and the labor market
- ▼ Learn about education and training possibilities

The best place to start, of course, is with your own school guidance office, but there are several ways to locate other professionals who may be helpful:

- ▼ Contact your local adult education program, college, or university.
- ▼ Call your local state employment service.
- ▼ Visit your local library and look through professional association guides.
- ▼ Look through the *Yellow Pages* telephone directory for counselors in private practice or for community agencies that provide career or job-training services.
- ▼ Call the director of your State Occupational Information Coordinating Committee. Each state has one, and you can reach the director through your state government. You can reach the National Occupational Information Coordinating Committee by calling 202/653-5665.

▼ Contact the National Board of Certified Counselors for a list of certified career counselors in your area and for consumer guidelines for selecting a career counselor. Send a self-addressed stamped (two postage stamps) envelope to:

National Board for Certified Counselors, Inc.
3-D Terrace Way, Greensboro, NC 27403
Phone 910/547-0607 Fax 910/547-0017

▼ Contact the International Association of Counseling Services (IACS). IACS accredits career counseling agencies throughout the United States and Canada. For a list of accredited agencies in your area, send a self-addressed stamped envelope to:

IACS
101 South Whiting Street, Suite 211
Alexandria, VA 22304
Phone 703/823-9840

In summary, by following the steps in this book and creating your own personal portfolio, you will:

▼ Learn more about yourself, your interests, and your goals

▼ Guide yourself through the process of planning your education and your career

▼ Create a place to record information about your past, current, and future education and work

▼ Store and organize important education- and work-related information

Part 1

INFORMATION ON WHO I AM

The activities in this section will help you find answers to the question, "Who am I?" You will gather information that can help you:

- ▼ Understand who you are and how you operate
- ▼ Examine your skills and abilities
- ▼ Learn from all areas of your life
- ▼ Discover how you change and grow
- ▼ Define your life roles as you change and grow

You are a unique person with your own interests, abilities, and values. Gathering information about yourself is a first step on the road to a satisfying career.

- ▼ What are your interests?
- ▼ What's important to you in your work?
- ▼ What skills, strengths, and experience do you have?
- ▼ What is your preferred work style?
- ▼ How do you handle stress?
- ▼ What do you need to grow and develop?

Knowing the answers to these questions will help you plan your education, choose a career direction, and persuade employers to hire you. The time and effort you put into this process is a worthwhile investment in your future.

Essential Portfolio Data

Do you know who you are? It may sound like a simple question, and the answer may be obvious for you; or the answer may be painfully elusive. How many of us really take the time to thoroughly examine our values and our goals? Unfortunately, that process can take a lifetime, and many people never find a satisfactory answer to the basic question, "Who am I?"

Having a good sense of *self* will help you in all aspects of your life's work.

Perhaps the most time-consuming portion of creating your own portfolio is locating and gathering personal information about yourself. But it is also the most critical. You will be asked to provide this information whenever you fill out a job application or go to an interview. Employment laws vary from state to state, so you may not be asked to provide all of the information listed on the worksheet; but you should be prepared to provide the information if you are asked.

Yet, knowing who you are and what you want in life will help you establish your goals and keep you focused on achieving them. A good place to start is to document your personal information. In this information superhighway cyberspace-technology computer age, our personal information may not seem so personal, as more and more people can easily gain access to our once-private records. In fact, your personal information may seem like mere statistical data. But as you fill out the following worksheets, you will begin to see yourself as others see you. What kind of impact does your name on a piece of paper have? Well, it all depends. It depends on whether the piece of paper is a loan approval or a warrant for your arrest. Bits and pieces of your personal information alone may not say much about you, but if you put the pieces together, a bigger picture begins to develop. In these worksheets, you will begin to put your pieces of data together to see what your information says about you.

TIP

If you want to preserve your certificates and other documents in good condition, you should make photocopies of the originals and place the copies in your portfolio.

INFORMATION ON
WHO I AM

Your Personal Information

Filling out this worksheet is the first step in creating your portfolio. Because your portfolio is where you will keep all your career and education information, it is a good idea to include items that help you make career decisions, put together a resume, and prepare for interviews. So you may want to include in your portfolio copies of the following items:

- ▼ Birth certificate
- ▼ Health records
- ▼ Picture identification or current photo
- ▼ Social Security card

- ▼ Passport
- ▼ Driver's license
- ▼ Work permit
- ▼ Noncitizen status papers
- ▼ Surveys, tests, or assessments results

Storing copies of these documents in your portfolio keeps this information at your fingertips when you need it.

My Personal Information

Full Name _____

Other Names I Have Used _____

Street Address _____

City _____ State/Province _____ Zip _____

Previous Address _____

City _____ State/Province _____ Zip _____

E-Mail Address _____

Telephone Numbers: Home _____ Work _____

Pager _____ Cell Phone _____

Mailing Address (if different) _____

City _____ State/Province _____ Zip _____

Social Security Number _____ Driver's License Number _____

Date of Birth _____ Place of Birth _____

U.S. Citizen? (Y/N) _____ If not, current status _____

Visa _____ Registration Number _____

Your Life Values

Many people believe that who you are is a reflection of what you value. Sociologists spend a lot of time debating whether we learn our values from our environments or whether we come genetically programmed with them. We won't try to answer that here. Suffice it to say that what you value is what motivates you. What you value in your life, education, and work has an impact on your career. If people are doing work they value, they are more committed to doing a good job. If you can balance what's important in your life with your work, you will find satisfaction both on and off the job. Some work values are listed below:

▼ Income level

▼ Work environment

▼ Team work

▼ Independent work

▼ Competition

▼ Structure and security

▼ Helping others

▼ Safety

▼ New skills development

▼ Change and variety

▼ Creativity

▼ Advancement

▼ Physical challenges

▼ Taking risks

This is only a sample list. Values are unique to every person. Each of us has different ideas about what's important in our work. Other life values outside of work might include these:

▼ Fun

▼ Hobbies or sports

▼ Community activities

▼ Family

▼ Friendships

▼ Religious activities

If you have difficulty identifying what you value, talk with a close friend or family member. Self-assessment instruments also can help you discover more about your values. Your school counselor may have several types of self-scoring instruments. Or check with a local adult education center, college, or university. Often these assessments are provided free or for a nominal fee.

INFORMATION ON
WHO I AM

What You Stand For

Another way of identifying your values is to make a list of the things that have been important to you in your school career. For example, is it important to you to make good grades? Do you want to take really challenging courses, even if it means you may earn a lower grade? Then list the things that are important to you outside of school. Now think about unpleasant experiences you would like to avoid in the future. List these on a separate sheet of paper. Share your lists with your parents, counselor, or friends who know you well. Do your lists reflect what they know about you? Be sure your lists contain items that *you* think are important, not what others say *should be* important. Divide the items into three categories: *must have, would like to have,* and *could do without for the right opportunity.* These categories relate to values that you would like a job to include.

From your *must have* and *would like to have* lists, select your 10 most important values. Write them in order of importance in the space provided here. You may not find many career options that match all of your values. But for an occupation to be satisfying, it should fulfill many of your important values.

As you explore career options, match what you have learned about your values to the descriptions of the occupations. As you talk to employers and interview for jobs, compare your list of values to what the job offers.

What I Stand For

The 10 values/beliefs that are most important to me:

1. _____
2. _____
3. _____
4. _____
5. _____
6. _____
7. _____
8. _____
9. _____
10. _____

INFORMATION ON
WHO I AM

Your Learning Style

Have you heard the term *lifelong learning?* It means that you don't stop learning when you finish school. Because of new technology, the way you do your job and live your life will constantly and rapidly change. To keep up with these changes, you will need to learn new skills both on and off the job.

People learn in different ways. Think about your best learning experience. What made it successful? Knowing how you learn best and choosing an occupation or training that matches your learning style increase your chances of success.

My Learning Style

(Check as many as apply.) When faced with something new, I learn best by:

_____   Reading about it

_____   Seeing it

_____   Seeing someone do it

_____   Listening to someone explain it

_____   Doing it myself

_____   Working with a small group to figure it out

_____   Other (explain) _____

_____

_____

_____

_____

_____

_____

_____

_____

INFORMATION ON **WHO I AM**

Your Personality Style

It is important that you think about your personality and temperament when exploring and choosing an occupation. Consider the following:

If you like . . .	Do not select an occupation in which you . . .
Change and variety in your work	Do the same tasks day after day
Meeting and talking with people	Work alone in an office
Planning your activities	Have constant interruptions

In reviewing your personality, you may discover areas you would like to work on or develop more fully. As people mature and grow, their personalities can and do change.

Your counselor's office may offer personality tests and temperament checklists. If not, look through the resource sections in this book; many of these resources are available at your local library or can be ordered from a bookstore. Make sure the tests you use provide information related to career choices.

My Personality Style

Think about how you behave, how you react to school or work situations, and how others see you. Then record this information below.

I would describe my personality or temperament as: _____

_____

_____

People who have known me for a long time would describe my personality as: _____

_____

_____

When others meet me for the first time, they would describe my personality as: _____

_____

_____

Personal Management Strategies

Your personal management style is how you handle life: how you approach risks, the ways you manage your time, how you deal with stress, the methods you use to stay healthy, and the ways you gain support. These are important factors to consider when you think about your education, when you choose a career direction, and when you want to tell an employer about your personal strengths on the job.

Your personal management style will influence how you manage circumstances in your job. Answering the following questions will help you determine if your management style is working well for you. If you aren't entirely satisfied with how you handle events in your life, you are not alone. Most of us can find areas to improve. The good news is that personal management styles can be learned. If your current strategies aren't working, think about trying some new ones. Talk with people you admire. Ask them how they manage their lives and their jobs. Your local library or bookstore also offers many resources that deal with coping with everyday life.

Managing your personal life makes it easier for you to manage your education and career. Perhaps someday you will even manage others in their careers. Do you see yourself in a leadership position? Think about some of your personal achievements and read the questions below. If you answer yes to two or more questions, perhaps you should consider a leadership role at some point in your career.

▼ Do you like to take responsibility for projects or groups of people?

▼ Can you delegate tasks and still maintain control?

▼ Do you see the problems of those around you as a challenge?

▼ Can you keep a positive attitude under stressful circumstances?

▼ Are you even-tempered, even when you are angry or provoked?

▼ Can you communicate in a way that motivates others?

▼ When you see something that needs to be done, do you do it yourself?

▼ Do you enjoy taking responsibility, solving problems, or working with others to achieve results?

Good managers can analyze situations and choose a course of action that is likely to achieve good results. Whether you manage other people or just yourself, it's important to have strategies that help you achieve good results in all areas of your life.

INFORMATION ON
WHO I AM

Your Risk-Taking Style

For some people, starting a new class or training program, going into a new school or college, or looking for a new job is exciting. For others, these activities feel risky and cause anxiety.

As you think about your risk-taking style, ask yourself these questions:

▼ How much risk can I handle right now? How much risk do I want to handle in my career? In my first job?

▼ Is a situation risky because I don't know much about it? Can I talk to someone who has been through it so I can get firsthand information?

▼ How will I benefit from change? Is the benefit worth the risk? What will happen if I don't take this chance?

▼ What can I do to make the change less risky?

▼ Who can give me support and encourage me?

My Risk-Taking Style

Think about a time in your life when you were going through a lot of changes or were faced with a life-changing decision. Were you comfortable with the change? Did the decision come easily? Would you do anything differently if faced with the same situation? Now answer the questions below.

When faced with change, I prefer to: _____

_____

_____

_____

_____

I consider the following situations risky:

1. _____

2. _____

3. _____

4. _____

INFORMATION ON
WHO I AM

Your Time Management Style

Planning your education or training, exploring different careers, and looking for work all require time and energy. For many of us, the time must be carved out of an already busy schedule. How well you manage your time affects your career planning and your performance on the job. Here are some questions you should ask yourself:

▼ Am I satisfied with how I manage my time both in and out of school? If not, how can I improve my time management skills?

▼ What am I allowing to get in the way of accomplishing what is important to me?

▼ Do I usually spend enough time on my high-priority activities?

If you are not satisfied with how you manage your time, meet deadlines, or accomplish your goals, there are many books and tapes you can check out for help. Check the resources at the end of this section or ask your school librarian for suggestions.

My Time Management Style
Answer the following questions to determine your time management style. A balance of school, home, and leisure activities offers the most satisfaction and helps reduce time management stress.

When there are a lot of demands on my time, I manage my time by: _____

_____

_____

_____

_____

_____

When faced with deadlines, I usually: _____

_____

_____

_____

_____

_____

Take Good Care of Yourself

Your health can have a big impact on what you do with your life and your career decisions. While there are some health conditions you can't control, there are many you can. One important factor that affects your overall health is stress. Prolonged stress has a harmful effect on your body. Stress can affect your immune system. Quite simply, stress can make you sick!

Change is usually stressful. Psychologists list the death of a loved one, divorce, and financial troubles at the top of the list of stress-producers. Another major stressor is job change. People who lose a job or face an uncertain future often experience more health problems than usual. They also tend to have more accidents during this time. In their book *Beat Stress with Strength*, Stefanie Spera and Sandra Lanto maintain that job satisfaction, or the lack of it, is the area where most people experience work-related stress. But complete job satisfaction is rare, because there are at least some disadvantages to almost every position in any given career. Knowing the disadvantages of a job and being prepared to deal with them are important parts of planning your career and your life's direction. If you're faced with accepting or staying in a job that gives you no satisfaction, you should consider the following:

> Exercise your mind and body to relieve stress, prohibit illness, and enhance your appearance.

▼ Do the advantages of the position outweigh the disadvantages?

▼ Is there something you can do to change the situation?

▼ Is it likely the situation will change if you do nothing and wait it out?

▼ Is your attitude toward the situation likely to change?

▼ Is the job a step in your long-term career plan?

Many times a situation appears hopeless until you step back and reevaluate it objectively. If you can't be objective, talk with other people whose opinions you value and trust. There are also many books available to help you identify and deal with stress. Check the resource list at the end of this section.

Taking care of your body and emotional health, and getting support when you need it, will also help you manage life's changes. To relieve stress and reduce health risks, experts recommend a four-part approach to wellness:

1. Eat a well-balanced diet.
2. Engage in regular physical exercise.
3. Find practical and emotional support.
4. Use healthy coping strategies.

Each of these topics is presented separately in the following pages.

Your Wellness Strategies

Eating Well

Machinery cannot operate without fuel, and your body cannot function well unless you provide it with a healthy, balanced diet. If you want help eating well, ask for advice from an expert:

▾ Your doctor

▾ The health teacher at your school

▾ The nutritionist at a local hospital or county health department

Most of us know the basic guidelines for healthy eating. You've probably heard the warnings about the effects of too much or too little fat, fiber, salt, iron, vitamins, caffeine, and cholesterol. Doctors and medical researchers have consistently linked poor diet to poor health. Take a quick trip to the bookstore, and you'll find entire shelves of cookbooks devoted to special nutritional needs: the low-fat diet, the low-salt diet, the low-sugar diet, the high-fiber diet, and the vegetarian diet, to name just a few. Education and common sense should dictate which nutrients your body requires to keep you "energized" for life.

CAUTION

Before starting any special diet or exercise program, consult your doctor or a certified professional nutritionist or trainer to determine the best course of action for your body's needs.

Being Physically Active

Physical exercise helps stretch and ease tense muscles. Exercising also uses the excess adrenaline your body produces when it is under stress. Exercise produces chemicals called endorphins that ease tension, improve your mood, and create feelings of well-being (sort of a natural tranquilizer without the side effects that pills produce).

Regular exercise helps your body's defenses ward off illnesses, including stress. Keeping physically fit helps you keep mentally fit. Being of sound mind and body is not just a popular saying, it's your best resource to keep up with the rigorous demands placed on you in everyday life. Before starting on any exercise program, you should talk to your doctor to help you determine the best type of activity for your body's needs.

Finding Practical and Emotional Support

Deciding on your education and career goals isn't something you have to do alone. It is easier to make good decisions and to cope with the stress if you get help. There are people (and resources) in your community who can provide the support and information you need, including these:

▼ Books or pamphlets on how to fill out job applications, write resumes or cover letters, and prepare for interviews

▼ School counselors and librarians who can provide information about occupations and the local job market

▼ Friends or family members who might offer guidance, financial assistance, and other help

▼ People you can ask about careers and job openings

People who are in the middle of a job search often describe it as being on an emotional roller coaster. Feelings of anticipation, fear, hope, disappointment, and excitement are all normal when you have a big decision to make.

Regardless of the situation, most of us find it helpful to talk about our feelings. We feel better, think more clearly, and act more effectively. Unfortunately, those who are closest to us often share our concerns. They may not be the good objective listeners they have been in the past. For emotional support, talk to people who

▼ Can listen to your feelings

▼ Care about you, but aren't emotionally involved in your situation

▼ Know how to give encouragement

▼ Have a positive attitude

▼ Believe in you and know what you can do

No one person can provide all of the support you need. Think about your current support network and how you might expand it. Your friends and schoolmates are probably going through the same experience. Or talk to your guidance counselor or someone who is trained to give you the emotional support and encouragement you need.

Using Effective Coping Methods

People have various ways of coping with change, stress, and uncertain times. Some methods are more helpful than others. Eating well, exercising, and getting support are some of the most effective ways of coping with change. However, some people find themselves acting in ways that only add to their problems: abusing alcohol or other drugs, overeating, not eating, staying in bed all day, or losing control of angry feelings and acting out in violent ways are signals that a person isn't coping well. You can learn ways to cope differently. Agencies, people, or programs that can help are available in your school or your community and are listed in your telephone book.

INFORMATION ON
WHO I AM

My Wellness Strategies

Take a few minutes to think about your health, how you handle stress, and what you do to cope. Fill in your thoughts below.

Physical Health

My current physical health situation: _____
_____

Concerns about my physical health: _____
_____
_____

Things I could do to help: _____
_____
_____

Mental/Emotional Health

My current mental/emotional health situation: _____
_____

Concerns about my emotional health: _____
_____
_____

Things I could do to help: _____
_____

Support Network

People I can talk to when I need to make a decision: _____
_____
_____
_____

Stress Management

I feel stressed by: _____
_____

Negative ways I deal with stress: _____
_____
_____

Positive ways I deal with stress: _____
_____
_____

Balancing Life Roles

Your many roles in life may include child, student, worker, sibling, partner, or even parent. As you grow and mature, your life changes and your roles change. Sometimes you may be focused on only one role. At other times, you may switch back and forth among many roles.

Your beliefs about what is important to you, your family background or culture, and your life events shape the choices you make on how to spend your time and energy. As you think about your life roles, ask yourself the following questions:

▼ How has my gender affected the roles I have chosen for myself?

▼ Has my cultural or ethnic background determined what I am expected to do? If so, how?

▼ Does my family have rules about who should do what? If so, what are the rules?

▼ Are there current family realities (such as a pregnancy or child, aging parents, a divorce, or financial difficulties) to which I must respond? What are the realities, and how do they affect the roles I have now?

▼ Are there other factors that affect the roles I have had in the past, have now, or expect to have in the future?

In the worksheets that follow, you will examine the various roles you've had in your life—and even the roles you think you might have in the future. Sometimes we define ourselves and who we are simply by our roles and what we do. Our work and our roles become so interchangeable we find it hard to separate one from the other. But it's important to reach a balance among your roles. Knowing the roles you play is essential to achieving personal satisfaction from your life's work.

Creating Your
**HIGH
SCHOOL
PORTFOLIO**

INFORMATION ON
**WHO I
AM**

Your Life Roles

As you plan your career, you need to take into account the many roles you have had in the past, the roles you have now, and the roles you expect to have in the future. Your life roles affect your career planning by:

▼ Determining how you spend your time and energy

▼ Providing experiences and developing skills

▼ Opening doors to some opportunities and closing doors to others

▼ Influencing some of the choices you think you can make

▼ Providing information you should consider as you decide on career paths and occupational choices

My Life Roles

List the roles you've had in the past, the roles you have now, and the roles you expect to have in the future.

Roles I've had in the past: _____

_____

_____

_____

Roles I have now: _____

_____

_____

_____

Roles I expect to have in the future: _____

_____

_____

_____

_____

Factors That Shape Your Life Roles

Many factors influence your life roles: your immediate and extended family; the relationships you have now; the place where you grew up; the things you do for fun and leisure; and your values, interests, work, ethnic background, and gender.

If you need help sorting out your thoughts about your roles, talk with a close friend, your parents, or your school counselor, or consult with any of the sources of extra help listed in the resources at the end of Part 1.

Factors That Shape My Life Roles

Describe how each of these factors has shaped your life roles.

My gender: _____

_____

_____

My cultural or ethnic heritage: _____

_____

_____

My childhood family and relationships: _____

_____

_____

My current family and relationships: _____

_____

_____

Other factors: _____

_____

_____

INFORMATION ON
**WHO I
AM**

Your Life Roles Pie Chart

In addition to identifying the roles you have, it's important to think about balancing those roles. Whether you are thinking of continuing your education beyond high school or entering the job market directly after high school, you will have to make room in your life for a new role. Look at your present roles in the list you made earlier. Think about how much time and energy each one takes. Divide the circle below into slices like a pie, with each of your present roles as a slice. The bigger the role in terms of the time and energy it requires, the bigger the slice of pie. As you look at your pie chart, what do you notice? Which of your life roles have the greatest priority? How do you balance your roles?

My Life Roles Pie Chart

INFORMATION ON
WHO I AM

Thinking About Your Life Roles

Now that you have looked at your past, current, and future roles and how your roles balance, ask yourself the following questions and record your answers on a separate sheet.

▼ Which roles can help me make changes I want to make? Which roles give the skills, experiences, and personal strengths I need to make changes? Which roles can help me reach my goals?

▼ Which roles are restricting my education or career planning goals right now?

▼ Do I want to make changes in the roles I have now? How do I make the changes?

▼ What new roles will I have in the future? Will they help me or hinder me?

▼ Am I satisfied with the balance of roles in my life?

▼ Do I think about my goals and dreams for the future as I take on new roles?

▼ Do I automatically take on roles without thinking about how they might affect what I want for myself? Do I take on roles simply because others expect me to assume them?

Thinking About My Life Roles

Take a moment to review how your roles affect your decisions. Reflect on how your roles have given you skills to handle changes in your life.

These roles help me as I look at education and career decisions: _____

_____

_____

_____

_____

These roles get in the way of education and career decisions: _____

_____

_____

_____

_____

I can make these roles work for me in the future by: _____

_____

_____

_____

_____

Your Interests

You will enjoy your career and your life much more if you find your job interesting. Career development experts list 12 general classifications of interest. Knowing which of these interests are attractive to you is an important part of finding the right career.

If you want to explore your career interests further, ask your counselor for an interest survey, or check with one of the sources of help listed at the end of this section. You'll find information about how your interests match different occupations in *The Complete Guide for Occupational Exploration.* This book, which is based on data from the U.S. Department of Labor and published by JIST Works, lists jobs classified within the 12 major occupational interest areas. For each job, *The Complete GOE* provides the following information:

▼ A description of job tasks

▼ The academic and vocational skills needed to perform the job

▼ Aptitudes and temperaments needed to perform the job

▼ Industries in which the job is found

▼ Training and educational requirements

▼ Physical demands

▼ Work environment descriptions

Your Career Interests

Read the descriptions of the 12 interest areas on the following worksheet. Select and number the three that you find the most interesting. Put a 1 by the area that interests you most, a 2 by the next most interesting, and a 3 by your third choice. Keep your interests in mind as you look at career possibilities. You also should consider areas that might interest you if you learned more about them. When you have finished filling out the worksheets in this book, you will have a much better idea of your skills, experiences, values, and other traits that support your career decision.

My Career Interests

My main interests are in the following areas (number your top three choices):

_____ **Art:** I like to express my feelings and my ideas in creative ways. I would like working in a creative way with images, words, art, music, drama, or dance.

_____ **Science:** I like discovering, collecting, and analyzing information about the natural world. I would like applying scientific research findings to problems in medicine, the life sciences, or the natural sciences.

_____ **Plants and animals:** I like working with plants and animals. I like working outdoors in all kinds of weather. I would like working in farming, forestry, or fishing.

_____ **Protection:** I like using authority to protect people and property. I would like working in law enforcement, fighting fires, or responding to emergency situations.

_____ **Mechanics:** I like applying mechanical principles to practical situations by using machines or hand tools. I would like working in engineering, building things, operating vehicles, or working in a trade.

_____ **Industry:** I like concrete, repetitive, organized activities performed in a factory setting. I would like inspecting, operating machinery, sorting products, setting up machines to produce a product, or supervising others while they do these activities.

_____ **Business detail:** I like clearly defined, organized activities that require accuracy and attention to detail, primarily in an office setting. I would like record keeping, working with the public, operating a computer, or managing an office.

_____ **Sales:** I like persuading others to a particular point of view or convincing them to take a course of action. I would like working with people in a store or sales office, buying and selling products to make a profit, or working in advertising.

_____ **Service:** I like helping people on a one-to-one basis, catering to their wishes and needs. I would like working in a hotel, restaurant, or travel service, or helping others with grooming or personal health.

_____ **Humanity:** I like helping others with their mental, spiritual, social, physical, or vocational needs. I would like providing therapy, religious counseling, nursing services, rehabilitation, or welfare services.

_____ **Leadership and influence:** I like leading and influencing others, using verbal or numerical persuasion. I would like working in a professional setting in administration, management, finance, law, social research, public relations, or education.

_____ **Physical performance:** I like to perform physical activities before an audience. I would like working in athletics or sports or performing physical feats.

Who I Am Checklist

Most people change their career directions more than once in a lifetime. *Creating Your High School Portfolio* provides a structure for you to explore and learn the steps of career planning. Each time you or your situation changes, you can go back and follow these steps.

Experts have identified certain skills people need to be effective career planners. This section has helped you develop self-knowledge skills. Take a minute to check now to see how you've done.

Who I Am Checklist

Put a check mark by the items on the list that apply to you.

_____ I can describe what is important in my life.

_____ I can identify how I prefer to learn new things.

_____ I can identify my personality traits and interests.

_____ I can describe my strategies to manage risk, time, and my health.

_____ I show positive skills in dealing with stress.

_____ I understand the importance of documenting my learning.

_____ I can describe my personal qualities.

_____ I can show an understanding of myself.

_____ I can tell how my personal, school, and work roles change over time.

_____ I can tell how my gender and culture affect my career decisions.

_____ I can describe the effects of my childhood, my family, and my relation-ships on my career decisions.

INFORMATION ON
**WHO I
AM**

Your Journal Entry

Use this worksheet to write down anything about you that is important and makes you a unique individual. Remember, you won't have to share these comments with anyone, but you need to be as truthful with yourself as possible. The self-knowledge you have gained in this section will give you the tools you need to succeed throughout your career and life.

My Journal Entry

In the space below, write down what you have learned about yourself and how you can use this information in career planning.

Name: _____   Date: _____

Useful things to remember about who I am: _____

_____

_____

_____

_____

_____

_____

_____

_____

_____

_____

_____

_____

_____

_____

_____

_____

_____

_____

List of Resources

Assessment Devices

The Armed Services Vocational Aptitude Battery (ASVAB). Administered at your local U.S. Military Entrance Processing Command.

Canfield, Albert A. *Learning Styles Inventory (LSI)*. Los Angeles: Western Psychological Services.

The COPES Work Values Survey. San Diego: Edits.

Farr, J. Michael. *Occupational Clues: A Career Interest Survey*. Indianapolis: JIST Works.

Holland, John L. *Self-Directed Search*™. Odessa, Florida: Psychological Assessment Resources.

Liptak, John J. *The Career Exploration Inventory (CEI)*. Indianapolis: JIST Works.

Liptak, John J. *Leisure Work/Search Inventory (LSI)*. Indianapolis: JIST Works.

Associations

American Counseling Association, 5999 Stevenson Avenue, Alexandria, VA 22304. http://www.counseling.org/

American Vocational Association, 1410 King Street, Alexandria, VA 22314. 800/826-9972. http://www.avonline.org/

National Career Development Association, 5999 Stevenson Avenue, Alexandria, VA 22304. 703/823-9800. http://www.uncg.edu/-eruccas2/ncda/

National Occupational Information Coordinating Committee, 2100 M Street, NW, Suite 156, Washington, DC 20037. 202/653-7680. http://www.noicc.gov/

Books

Bridges, William. *Surviving Transition*. New York: Doubleday.

The Complete Guide to Occupational Information. Indianapolis: JIST Works.

Lakein, Alan. *How to Get Control of Your Time and Your Life*. New York: McKay.

McGee-Cooper, Ann. *Time Management for Unmanageable People*. New York: Bantam.

Pennebaker, J. *Opening Up: The Healing Power of Confiding in Others*. New York: Morrow.

Sher, Barbara, and Anne Gottlieb. *Wishcraft: How to Get What You Really Want*. New York: Ballantine.

Spera, Stefanie, and Sandra Lanto. *Beat Stress with Strength: A Survival Guide for Work and Life*. Indianapolis: JIST Works.

Young Person's Occupational Outlook Handbook: Descriptions for America's Top 250 Jobs. Indianapolis: JIST Works.

Computer Software

Corderman, Patricia Waidren, and Marilyn Maze. *Career Finder, 1996-1997 Edition*. New Orleans: Winter Green Orchard House.

Crystal-Barkely Corporation and Eric O. Sandburg. *Career Design Software*. Sedona, AZ: Careers by Design.

JIST's Multimedia Occupational Outlook Handbook, Second Edition. Indianapolis: JIST Works.

JIST's Electronic Occupational Outlook Handbook, Second Edition. Indianapolis: JIST Works.

Part 2

WHAT I CAN DO

Now that you have had a chance to take a look at who you are, the next step is to explore what you can do—or what skills you can offer a prospective employer. One thought an employer has when hiring someone is, "What does this person have to offer in the way of educational background, skills, knowledge, ability, and past experience?"

What Can You Offer?

Your experiences, skills, and accomplishments can all give you clues to future occupations. That's because it is often easier to build a career direction on what you already know. They also show an employer what you have to offer.

It's important to keep records of what you have done and what you have learned. These records will help you choose a career, put together a resume, fill out job applications, and prepare for interviews. Take some time to gather the following documents and put them, or copies of them, in your portfolio.

- ▼ Grade reports
- ▼ Transcripts
- ▼ Certificates
- ▼ Diplomas
- ▼ Performance reports
- ▼ Awards
- ▼ Licenses

- ▼ Test results
- ▼ Letters
- ▼ Job appraisals
- ▼ Slides
- ▼ Photos
- ▼ Resumes

You should also include the following documentation in your portfolio as you accumulate it in the future:

- ▼ Workshops completed
- ▼ Languages learned or spoken
- ▼ Home activities
- ▼ Hobbies
- ▼ Favorite school subjects
- ▼ Continuing Education Units (CEUs)
- ▼ Things you've taught yourself

- ▼ Apprenticeships
- ▼ Military training
- ▼ Courses completed
- ▼ On-the-job training/education
- ▼ Volunteer service
- ▼ Internships
- ▼ General Educational Development certificate (GED certificate)

Do not underestimate the skills you have to offer. People develop skills and build expertise from all parts of their lives. You can do a lot more than you think!

You might also include any material or stories from your life that show what you've learned in school or from someone else. This could include what you have done at school, on the job, in your home, or in the community. It might even be something you did just for yourself.

Write down on extra sheets of paper everything you can remember about the many things you have done. As you review your list and documentation, you may see similar skills and kinds of experiences occurring again and again. Pay attention to these important patterns as you look at future careers.

If you need help finding patterns or matching your past and present to a future career, ask your school career counselor to help you (or get help from another trained professional; see the list of resources at the end of this section).

Your Work Experience

If you think the only work you should include in your portfolio is your paid work experience, you are underestimating what you have to offer. A person develops skills and builds experience from every part of his or her life, whether or not it is work-related.

Employers want to know not only what you have done but how well you have done it. And it's up to you to communicate your skills to the employer or interviewer. One of the most important things you can do before deciding on a career (and, consequently, on your education path) is to identify all your skills. Once you've done that, you can emphasize your most valuable skills to an employer or interviewer.

When you record your achievements, you will not only have a portfolio, but also raise your self-esteem and boost your confidence levels.

As you review your experience in this section, remember to include in your portfolio any commendations, awards, letters of recognition, performance evaluations, and positive comments from teachers, supervisors, coworkers, customers, or clients.

In the worksheet that follows, you'll have a chance to list your responsibilities and skills from any jobs you've held. Be sure to write as much about the tasks as possible. This will help you decide which tasks were your most important. If you need more space, continue describing your experience on a blank sheet of paper.

TIP

Before writing, make as many copies of the worksheet as you think you'll need, or use your own paper. (Keep the original page blank for future copying.)

WHAT I CAN DO

My Work Experience

When filling out this worksheet, describe as many of the tasks performed as you think will be helpful to you. Remember, work experience includes paid or unpaid, full- or part-time work.

Job title: _____

Employer/Organization

Name: _____

Phone/Fax: _____

Street address: _____

City/State/Zip: _____

Tasks performed: _____

_____

Skills required: _____

_____

Dates: _____

Person you can use as a reference: _____

Address: _____

Phone/Fax: _____

Job title: _____

Employer/Organization

Name: _____

Phone/Fax: _____

Street address: _____

City/State/Zip: _____

Tasks performed: _____

_____

Skills required: _____

_____

Dates: _____

Person you can use as a reference: _____

Address: _____

Phone/Fax: _____

WHAT I CAN DO

Your Home/Leisure/Community Activities

Activities you do in your free time are important clues that can lead to future occupations. You choose the activities to do around your home, for your community, and for other people in your leisure time because you like them. Think about whether you would like to do any of these activities in your career. Also, think about what skills you have developed that you would like to use in the future. Remember to include in your portfolio examples, photographs, programs, or other materials that show what you've learned or accomplished.

My Home/Leisure/Community Activities

List your home/leisure/community activities in the space provided below. After completing the statements, put a check mark beside those activities that you could do for pay. (Some examples of community activities include sports clubs, church activities, a political party, youth groups, and social clubs or organizations.)

At home, I do the following jobs: _____

_____

_____

_____

_____

In my spare time, I like to do these activities: _____

_____

_____

_____

_____

In my community, I am active in: _____

_____

_____

_____

_____

WHAT I CAN DO

What You're Proud Of

Often people take what they do for granted. They think everybody else can do the same thing and do it well. As you consider your career plans, you may focus on what went wrong in the past rather than what you have done well. Looking at what you've accomplished strengthens your self-confidence. It is also a good way to identify skills and abilities that will interest future employers.

Helping your friends, taking care of younger siblings, playing on a team, helping run a household, keeping fit, and staying healthy are as important as winning trophies. Don't underestimate the importance of what you have accomplished. In all of your experiences, look for the skills you have developed, such as these:

▼ Helping friends involves teamwork and problem-solving skills.

▼ Helping care for siblings requires people skills, responsibility, and dependability.

▼ Helping in a household involves budgeting, organization, and time management skills.

▼ Keeping fit and staying healthy demands energy, discipline, and motivation.

Things I've Done That Made Me Proud

List your accomplishments and what made you feel proud in the spaces provided. Be sure to consider all your life experiences.

I have accomplished these things in my life: _____

_____

_____

_____

_____

_____

_____

Here are three things I am really proud of:

1. _____

2. _____

3. _____

Identify Your Essential Skills

Young people looking for their first jobs often worry that employers won't think they have any skills because they have no previous work experience. The truth is that skills are developed in school, in volunteer work, and in the home. You have work skills that you use at home and home skills that you can use at work or in your community.

There are many different types of skills and many ways to classify them. For further reading on skills identification, check out the resources at the end of this section. It is important to know that a skill is simply something you can do well. And, more importantly, most people have hundreds of skills, not just a few.

In this book, skills are divided into four major areas:

1. **Personal:** These are the types of skills you can apply to various jobs. Sometimes they are called *personality traits* or self-management skills. Some examples of these skills include dependability, controlling one's temper, doing high-quality work, following safety standards, and honesty.

2. **Basic:** These are the everyday skills you use to get by and survive. Some examples include driving, reading, and following directions.

3. **Thinking:** These skills relate to your insight and ability to process information. V*isualizing* is a thinking skill. Visualizing means you have the ability to see, in your mind's eye, a finished product before it's put together. It also means you have the ability to imagine or predict what could result from taking a certain step or making a decision.

4. **Technical:** These relate directly to a certain job or type of job. Some examples of technical skills are operating a forklift, using a word processor, or keeping financial records.

You can apply all of these skills to new or existing jobs.

As you can see, skills can take on many different names and classifications. What is important, however, is that you learn to communicate your skills to other people.

If you need additional help in identifying and documenting your skills, many books and materials are available at your local library. Talk with your school counselor, your teachers, and your friends. Have them tell you what they think are your most visible skills. A good dictionary or thesaurus also is useful in finding definitions of other skill words that are unfamiliar to you.

What You Can Do

Look back at what you've done and what you've learned in school, in volunteer work, in paid jobs, and in your leisure time. Take some time to identify the skills you've developed. On a separate sheet of paper, write those skills down. Then think about the skills listed on the worksheet that follows and either write on the worksheet an example of how you have demonstrated that skill or put in your portfolio some documentation that shows how you have used the skill. Here are some examples:

Skill...	How You Have Used the Skill...
Self-management	I'm always on time for school. (Demonstration)
Negotiation	Chores contract I wrote with my parents. (Documentation)
Organization	I planned and organized all the activities for my high school prom. (Demonstration)
Diplomatic	I have served on my school's conflict mediation team, teaching other students conflict resolution skills. (Demonstration and documentation)
Hard working	I was Employee of the Month at my new job—the first part-time employee ever to receive the award. (Documentation)

Making a list of skills is a good starting point in identifying what you can do for an employer, but you must also practice speaking your new skills language. By thinking of all your skills and listing examples of how you have used them, you will learn to communicate your skills where it really counts—in a school or job interview. Try the following exercise at home. The next time you see a TV commercial advertising a product or service, think of your own experience with that product (or a similar one) and what skills you need to use that product or service. Look at the examples that follow.

Commercial Product or Service	Skills Associated with Product or Service
New car	Negotiation Manual dexterity Map reading Budgeting Mechanical ability
New cake or dessert mix	Reading a recipe Following directions Organizing work space Measuring Using appliances properly

There is a difference between what you *can* do and what you *actually* do.

Your skills make you a unique individual. They will change over time, and it is natural that you will continue to develop some skills more than others. Because of technological advances and changes in the workplace, you are likely to change jobs and careers more than once in your lifetime. Your ability to transfer your skills and adapt to a new career is very important. People who understand and communicate their skills well make job and career changes more easily than those who don't.

What I Can Do

Give an example of how you can show that you have these skills (documentation or demonstration). Put a check mark next to those skills you would like to improve.

Personal Skills

Self-management: _____

_____

Communication: _____

_____

Teamwork: _____

_____

Leadership: _____

_____

Negotiation: _____

_____

Problem solving: _____

_____

Listening: _____

_____

Budget management: _____

_____

Decision making: _____

_____

Other personal skills: _____

_____

_____

_____

WHAT I CAN DO

Basic Skills

Reading: _____

_____

Writing: _____

_____

Listening: _____

_____

Mathematics: _____

_____

Speaking: _____

_____

Computer literacy: _____

_____

Thinking Skills

Creative thinking: _____

_____

Critical thinking: _____

_____

Visualizing: _____

_____

Knowing how to learn: _____

_____

Reasoning: _____

_____

Analyzing: _____

_____

Technical Skills

(For example, welding, cooking, data entry, word processing, landscaping, surveying, nursing, and broadcasting)

_____

_____

_____

_____

_____

44

WHAT I CAN DO

Your Personal Qualities

In addition to skills, experience, training, and education, some of the most important things employers look for in the people they hire are personal qualities or strengths. People may have the skills to perform a job, but if they can't get to work on time, can't get along with others, can't be trusted to finish a job, or are dishonest, employers can't and won't hire them.

On the worksheet that follows, document or demonstrate that you have each quality listed. Use examples from school, home, or community activities. If you have trouble coming up with examples, it may indicate an area to work on to improve your employability, or you may need to talk with a friend, family member, or counselor who can help you identify your strengths.

My Personal Qualities

Give an example that reflects that you have these qualities (documentation or demonstration).

Responsibility: _____

Self-esteem: _____

Sociability: _____

Dependability: _____

Initiative: _____

Integrity/Honesty: _____

Cooperation: _____

Tolerance: _____

Persistence: _____

Flexibility: _____

Other: _____

_____

_____

WHAT I CAN DO

Adding Up Your Experiences

Throughout your life, you have probably done many things that have given you a great sense of accomplishment. They might have happened many years ago, or perhaps they occurred just yesterday. They might have been big things, or something small. You may have received personal recognition, or maybe you did not. What is important is that these accomplishments matter to you.

Your accomplishments can provide clues to your skills. The skills you used in achieving your accomplishments are the most powerful skills you possess. Chances are, you are good at and enjoy using these skills, too. If you can identify these skills and use them in your job, you will have a better chance at succeeding in your career, and you probably will gain greater satisfaction from doing that type of work. Simply put, often we are happiest and most successful when we are using our best skills.

As you review your school, work, volunteer, and other experiences, along with your accomplishments, skills, and personal qualities, you probably have learned some new things about yourself. Take a few minutes now and summarize this information in the space below.

Adding Up My Experiences

As I look at all I've learned and accomplished, I realize these new things about myself:

_____

_____

_____

_____

_____

_____

_____

_____

_____

_____

Challenges and Realities

One sure fact of life is that things constantly change. For many people, change is a challenge. It means letting go of the familiar and moving toward the unknown. You have experienced and managed many changes throughout your life. Some of these changes might include:

- Going to school for the first time
- Taking your first job
- Entering an intimate relationship
- Leaving an intimate relationship

- Moving
- Changing schools
- Having a baby
- Leaving home

> Take time to figure out what is getting in the way of reaching a goal, making a dream come true, or changing a situation you want to improve.

Whether you are contemplating going to college, attending a trade school, doing an apprenticeship, or entering the workforce directly after high school, you are facing a major change in your life. And change forces you to confront yourself and your abilities in a very basic way. Creating this portfolio is just one way of confronting yourself and examining all the possibilities open to you.

As a young adult, you may feel that you aren't free to make all the choices you would like—that responsibilities, money, and other realities limit your options. One of your tasks is to figure out what is getting in the way of reaching a goal, making a dream a reality, or changing a situation. Sometimes barriers are really what they appear to be—things you can't change. Then you have to make other choices. However, at times you may see only the barriers and not the possibilities. There may be ways to get over, under, around, or through a barrier if you think outside the box.

On a separate blank sheet of paper, take a few minutes to write down the barriers you believe are keeping you from making an important change in your life. Some examples might include:

- Fear of failure
- Fear that change will interfere with your personal relationships
- Feelings that change will create a hardship for others in your life

Does your barrier list include the word *fear*? No matter what type of change you are contemplating—career, schooling, relocating, or change of personal status—fear often accompanies change. In her book *Dare to Change Your Job and Your Life*, Carole Kanchier says this about fear:

> Fears often act as barriers to your progress. Growing, which is really just abandoning a comfortable position, usually involves pain. Trying to avoid pain by constructing rigid roles, defenses, viewpoints, or excuses only makes the process more difficult. The first and most important risk you can take is to be honest with yourself. Accept that you are afraid. Like all emotions, fear has a purpose; it alerts you to take action to protect yourself from loss.

The bottom line is that, in most cases, fear is a barrier to growth and success. By identifying your fears, you can deal with them openly and honestly. All of us have the capacity to unlearn our fear of change. Taking action to overcome your barriers is the first step.

On the worksheets that follow, you are asked to think about how you handle changes in your life. These exercises will help you further identify your strengths and limitations so you can learn to maximize your strengths and overcome your limitations.

WHAT I CAN DO

Your Personal Challenges

Think about all the changes you have made and the challenges you have met in your life. Knowing how you handled those changes can help you deal with future changes, as well as help you understand your reaction to change.

My Personal Challenges

Take a few minutes to review what has helped you manage change in the past. Also think about what you did that got in your way. What have you learned about how you handle change? Write that information in the space provided.

When I have had to change, the things that bothered me most were: _____

_____

_____

_____

Three things I never want to do again and why:

1. _____

2. _____

3. _____

Things that get in my way as I grow and change: _____

_____

_____

_____

Things that have excited me about change: _____

_____

_____

_____

What I have learned about myself from these challenges: _____

_____

_____

_____

WHAT I CAN DO

Your Personal Realities

Now that you have reviewed your challenges, it's time to think about your realities. If you think there is a barrier preventing you from making the changes you want or reaching your goals, ask yourself the following questions:

1. Is it a barrier I have built for myself? Is it really beyond my control?
2. Can I change my way of thinking about that barrier?
3. Are there ways around this barrier that I haven't considered?

On a separate sheet of paper, make a list of everything you can do to remove that barrier. Make the list as long as you can. Ask other people to help you expand your list. Write down even the ideas that sound silly or impossible. Sometimes a silly idea can be a key to a real answer. When you think your list is complete, discuss the ideas with your school counselor or with others and get their input. Pick one or two ideas and try them.

My Personal Realities

On this worksheet, record your realities. They may be listed already or they may be different. Some realities may be very strong points to help you change your career plans; others may be temporary barriers to your plans.

Budget: _____

_____

Appearance/Clothing: _____

_____

Family care responsibilities: _____

_____

Transportation: _____

_____

Education: _____

Other: _____

_____

How You Can Grow from Here

Life doesn't ever stand still. People change. The economy changes. Industries and employment opportunities change. Jobs come and go. Careers change. You are always faced with a choice: You can choose to stand still and be left behind, or you can choose to grow and pursue new opportunities.

So far, you've looked at yourself and what makes you tick. Now take some time to review what you have learned. Think about how this information affects your goals for your future and what you would like to do for your own growth. You may have discovered that you need new skills. You may have identified things you would like to change about your current situation or yourself. Record all these thoughts on the worksheet that follows.

> You can choose to stand still and get left behind, or you can choose to grow and pursue new opportunities.

One important thing to remember about change and growth is that you do not lose your skills when you change the way you apply them. It is equally important that you accept yourself, no matter what your limitations, if you are to achieve personal growth. If you are having trouble making a change or accepting your limitations, you will find several materials to help you work through these issues. Some are mentioned in the list of resources at the end of this section, and most of these you can find at your local library or bookstore. If you are afraid that your limitations are too great to overcome by yourself, ask your school counselor for help, or look in the *Yellow Pages* for a professional counselor.

CAUTION

Don't expect to change in all areas of your life at once. Trying to make too many changes at one time can be overwhelming. It can actually get in the way of your progress.

WHAT I CAN DO

How I Can Grow from Here

Take a few minutes now to record your thoughts on the worksheet below as you reflect on who you are. If you want to, you can create your own categories or use the space to fit your needs. Again, use whatever fits your style—including drawings, photos, or magazine pictures—to respond to the statements. Put a star by one or two items that you want to change. These personal goals will become part of your career plans.

What I'd like to learn: _____

_____

_____

_____

My dreams for the future: _____

_____

_____

_____

What I want out of life: _____

_____

_____

_____

Skills I'd like to master: _____

_____

_____

_____

Things I want to change about myself: _____

_____

_____

_____

Things I would like to do for my community: _____

_____

_____

_____

Knowing what I want will help me in my career decisions by: _____

_____

_____

_____

I can use this information in a job search or interview by: _____

_____

_____

WHAT I CAN DO

What You Can Do Checklist

Employers often select job seekers with less experience who present their skills well in an interview. For this reason, it is important that you can communicate your skills. This section has focused on identifying and developing your skills and abilities. Check now to see how you've done.

What I Can Do Checklist

Put a check mark next to the statements that apply to you.

_____ I can describe my career interests.

_____ I can describe ways to cope during change and transition.

_____ I know others who can help me make changes.

_____ I understand how I deal with change in my life.

_____ I know the personal realities that affect my decisions.

_____ I understand the importance of documenting my skills and abilities.

_____ I can identify my achievements related to school, work, and leisure.

_____ I can describe my different types of skills and what they are.

_____ I can show positive skills in dealing with others.

_____ I can tell how my relationships and leisure activities affect my career choices and other decisions.

_____ I can describe how my education, work, relationships, and leisure activities are all connected.

_____ I understand how to balance the demands of school, work, my relationships, and my leisure time.

WHAT I CAN DO

Your Journal Entry

Our accomplishments, as well as our failures, can be important clues to our skills and abilities. Most of us have experienced certain achievements that make us feel good about ourselves. When we succeed at something, it gives us more confidence to try something new. It is also important to recognize that setbacks can and do occur. However, failure and rejection can be overcome— they can even be good learning experiences.

My Journal Entry

In the space below, write down one accomplishment from any part of your life that has meant the most to you. Then write a detailed story about that accomplishment. Be sure to include as many factors as you can think of that contributed to your success. When you have finished, circle all the skills you used to accomplish your goal.

One accomplishment that is important to me:

_____

_____

_____

_____

_____

_____

_____

_____

_____

_____

List of Resources

Assessment Devices

Farr, J. Michael. *The Guide for Occupational Exploration Inventory*. Indianapolis: JIST Works.

Liptak, John J. *Barriers to Employment Success Inventory (BESI)*. Indianapolis: JIST Works.

Liptak, John J. *The Career Exploration Inventory (CEI)*. Indianapolis: JIST Works.

Liptak, John J. *Leisure Work/Search Inventory*. Indianapolis: JIST Works.

Match: Making a Terrific Career Happen. San Diego: Edits.

Books

Bolles, Richard Nelson. *What Color Is Your Parachute?* Berkeley, CA: Ten Speed Press.

Farr, J. Michael. *Getting the Job You Really Want,* Revised Edition. Indianapolis: JIST Works.

Farr, J. Michael. *The Guide for Occupational Exploration Inventory Crosswalks Book*. Indianapolis: JIST Works.

Farr, J. Michael. *The Right Job for You,* Second Edition. Indianapolis: JIST Works.

Krannich, Ronald L., and Caryl R. Krannich. *Discover the Best Jobs for You!* Second Edition. Manassas Park, VA: Impact Publications.

Shields, Nancy E. *Dictionary of Occupational Terms*. Indianapolis: JIST Works.

Tieger, Paul D., and Barbara Barron-Tieger. *Do What You Are*. Boston: Little, Brown.

Videos

Farr, J. Michael. *Identify Your Skills: A Job Search Essential*. Indianapolis: JIST Works.

Farr, J. Michael. *Skills Identification*. Indianapolis: JIST Works.

San Diego Department of Education. *Know Your Skills*. Indianapolis: JIST Works.

Part 3

EXPLORING CAREER OPTIONS

Now that you have had a chance to take a look at yourself, the next step is to look at the world of work. This section will be useful to you throughout your career. Whether you are looking for your first job, trying to move up in a company, or seeking a new job, the first step in the process is to research occupations and businesses that interest you. The world of work changes rapidly, and finding out about the changes in jobs is important. This involves a time commitment in doing the necessary research, but the payoff is a job that is right for you.

In Part 3, "Exploring Career Options," you will discover:

▼ How to locate and use career and educational information

▼ How your skills and abilities relate to the world of work

▼ What it takes to be self-employed

In this section, you will gather information about career possibilities, just as you gathered information about yourself and your abilities in the first two sections. Here you will research occupations, industries, and businesses, as well as your prospects for employment.

The Perfect Job for You

Earlier you spent time thinking about your values and interests; your experiences, skills, accomplishments, and personal management styles; and your life roles, challenges, and realities. Now you're going to put that information to work in choosing a career path.

But before you begin looking at career options, think about what your ideal job would be like—the job you've always wanted, the job that would meet most of your needs. Consider all that you know about yourself, close your eyes, and picture the "perfect" job. Then answer these questions:

Location: Where are you working?

▼ Is it in your own country?
▼ Is it in a foreign country?
▼ What region is it in?
▼ What is the climate?
▼ What is the size of the city?
▼ Is it in an urban or rural setting?

Work site: What does it look like?

▼ Is it inside or outside?
▼ Do you stay in one place or move around?
▼ What equipment does it have?
▼ What does the physical setting look like?
▼ Is it a big, midsize, or small company?
▼ What kind of clothes do you wear?
▼ Are you working at home?
▼ Is it your own business?

Tasks and responsibilities: What are you doing?

▼ Are you doing physical tasks? Mental tasks? A combination?
▼ Are you working with data and information? How much of the time?
▼ Are you working with people? How much of the time? How many people?
▼ Are you working with equipment? How much of the time?
▼ Are you a leader? A follower? A planner? A doer?
▼ What skills are you using?
▼ What is your typical day like?

Coworkers: With whom are you working?

▼ What kind of person is your boss?
▼ Are you the boss or a supervisor?
▼ What are your coworkers like?
▼ Are you part of a team?
▼ How many people work with you?
▼ Do you work alone?

Practically speaking, few people work in an occupation that is ideal in every way. But the more you focus on what you want, the more likely you are to get as close to your ideal as possible.

Your Ideal Job

Knowing your ideal job will help you discover what you want in your first job. This activity will help you stretch your thinking about career possibilities. As you gather information about possible jobs and occupations, compare that information with what is most important to you.

My Ideal Job

Take some time now to record your vision of your ideal job. Then judge each career possibility with your ideal job in mind.

My ideal job is one in which I: _____

_____

_____

_____

_____

_____

_____

_____

_____

_____

_____

_____

_____

_____

_____

_____

_____

_____

_____

_____

Career Exploration Activities

As you research career options, you may well feel overloaded with information about jobs, industries, statistics, and business opportunities. Newspapers, magazines, radio, television, your parents, your high school counselor, and your friends can all provide tidbits of information about different career opportunities and jobs. But do you know where they got their information? Is the information they are giving you current? How do you make sense of all this information?

Ask yourself these questions before relying on any information:

▼ **Is the information up-to-date?** A five-year-old survey of employers is not as reliable as one completed in the past year. Rapid changes in our economy and in technology can make career information obsolete within only one or two years. Sometimes there is a time lag between gathering and publishing survey results. Make sure you know when the data was gathered, so you can be sure you're getting the most current information possible.

▼ **Is the information accurate?** Some information passes through many sources. In doing so, it can become misinterpreted or made downright wrong. When you hear, see, or read information, ask these questions: What is the source of this information? Does the source really know? Is this an opinion, or is it based on real data?

▼ **Is the information unbiased?** For example, if you talk with people who are not happy in their jobs, you may get information that has a negative slant. Ask yourself if the source of information is objective.

▼ **Is the information confirmed by many sources?** Another way to judge information is seeing, hearing, and reading the information in many sources. For example, you may talk with five different people about the same career area. If most of the information is the same, you can more comfortably rely on that information. Or you might read government data, use a computerized system at the library, and talk with your school counselor. If all sources confirm what you've heard, then your confidence in that information increases.

CAUTION

Do not disregard a major career interest simply because you uncover some negative information. At this point, you are exploring all your interests. If the career truly interests you, expand your research until you are satisfied you have all the information you need to make an informed and responsible career decision. Remember, trust your own judgment above all else.

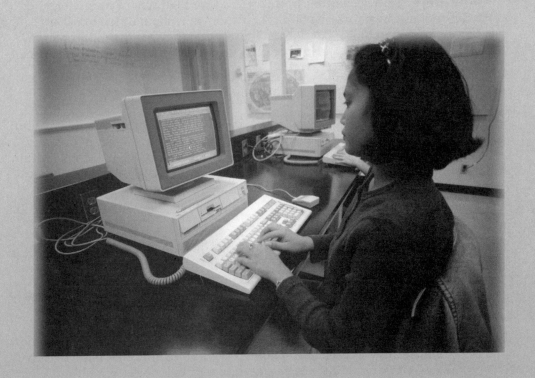

Your Career Exploration Checklist

As you research information on career options, some of the terms you encounter may be new to you. Here are some explanations.

Informational interviews. This means talking with people who are doing the job you're interested in, to ask questions about what they do. The purpose is to gain information, *not* to interview for a job opening. Here are some questions you might ask in an informational interview:

▼ What are the major tasks of the job?

▼ What training or education is necessary?

▼ What is the work environment like?

▼ What is the pay range (for both entry-level and experienced workers)?

▼ What are the positives about this work? What are the negatives?

▼ Who else should I talk to about this occupation?

Job shadowing. This is an excellent way to see firsthand what a person in a job really does. You "go to work" with someone for a day, a few days, or even a week to observe all the aspects of that occupation.

Job clubs. You can find these programs in community organizations, government agencies, outplacement firms, or maybe at your own school. Job clubs train people how to effectively look for work and locate and contact employers. A club also provides practical help, such as a base for job hunting, employer listings, and office equipment. Program leaders and other job seekers provide structure, emotional support, and encouragement.

Career information software. Computerized information systems may be available at your library, your high school, a nearby college, or the local state employment office. Ask your guidance counselor for help in finding and using one. Many systems match information about you to possible occupations. Some provide information about occupations, such as descriptions; skills, training, or education required; pay ranges; and related jobs.

Career resource centers. The most convenient one, of course, is the one at your own school. But if you want to broaden your options, or if your school does not offer a career resource center, check with local large businesses, colleges and universities, libraries, or government or community agencies. These centers provide many sources of information in one place, including books, journal articles, microfiche, video/audio tape, CD-ROMs, and computer diskettes.

Internet. Search the Web for career and job-related sites. Your librarian can help you.

Outplacement centers. These often share job openings and employer lists, and provide resume-writing assistance, interview training, and career coaching.

TIP

As you learn about careers, you might want to keep track of the information you gather on the "My Career Exploration Worksheet." Make copies of this checklist and the worksheet, as you will need one of each per occupation that interests you.

My Career Exploration Checklist

Occupation: _____

The career exploration activities on this checklist will give you an idea of how and where to gather the information you need. You should add other activities as you discover them. Be sure to fill in the name of the person you call, specify where to call, and give yourself a deadline to make that contact. Then meet your deadlines!

✔ Activity	Whom/Where to Call	When
❏ Talk with family and friends (network)		
❏ Talk to your school counselor		
❏ Do research at the library		
❏ Use the Internet		
❏ Join a career-related organization		
❏ Schedule informational interviews		
❏ Write for information on occupations		
❏ Job shadow		
❏ Visit the job service office		
❏ Volunteer		
❏ Join a job club		
❏ Go for job interviews		
❏ Visit a job training office		
❏ Attend career days at local businesses		
❏ Attend career days at school		
❏ Check into adult education programs		
❏ Use career information software		
❏ Visit a career resource center		
❏ Go to an outplacement center		
❏ Other		

EXPLORING CAREER OPTIONS

Your Career Interests

Think about your skills, abilities, interests, and experiences. Then think about the kinds of jobs you could do with the skills you have now. What occupations do you have an interest in that you could do if you had more training, education, or work experience? On this worksheet, list the jobs you could do now, even if you aren't very enthusiastic about them. Then list jobs you have an interest in and could do with more education or training. You may want to work at an entry-level job to get the experience necessary to move on to the job you really want.

Now is the time to consider how you will get the education, training, or experience for the careers in which you're really interested. Generally, the more education or training you have, the more pay you receive. So it may be well worth the extra time and money to qualify yourself for a job in which your interest is high. (Section 4 will help you decide on your education and training options.)

Add more jobs as you do the activities in this section. Your interests could change as you discover more about certain jobs.

My Career Interests

In the left column, list the types of jobs you do with the skills and abilities you have now. In the right column, list the types of jobs you could do with more training, education, or experience.

Jobs I could get with the skills and knowledge I have now:

_____

_____

_____

_____

_____

_____

_____

_____

_____

_____

Jobs I could get with more training, education, or work experience:

_____

_____

_____

_____

_____

_____

_____

_____

_____

_____

Your Career Exploration Worksheet

When you are doing career exploration activities, you will gather information about specific jobs and occupations, such as:

▼ The nature of the work

▼ The industries that include these occupations

▼ Training or education required

▼ Working conditions

▼ Employment trends and advancement possibilities

▼ Related occupations

▼ How well your values, interests, education, skills, and abilities match

CAUTION

Just because you don't have the job qualifications, don't discard an occupational area in which you are truly interested. Instead, think about how you can get the education, training, or experience you need.

"My Career Exploration Worksheet" is a good place to keep track of all the details you learn about an occupation. One very good source of career information is the *Occupational Outlook Handbook* (*OOH*) published by the U.S. Department of Labor and revised every two years. An easy-to-use version geared especially to young people is the *Young Person's OOH* (published by JIST Works). Many computerized sources of career information include data from the *OOH*. Other resources are listed at the end of this section.

You will also research the labor market to find out:

▼ Employment trends (national, state, and local)

▼ Occupations and industries that are growing, staying the same, or declining

▼ Current or anticipated job openings

Since you will use many sources of information and look into a number of possibilities, use the following worksheet as a master copy and make extra copies. Be sure you file your worksheets in your portfolio. Also remember to file in your portfolio newspaper clippings, magazine articles, or pictures of career areas that interest you.

My Career Exploration Worksheet

Use this worksheet to track all your career research about a certain occupation. Before writing, make photocopies for each occupation that interests you.

Name of occupation: _____

Source of information: _____

What do workers in this job actually do? What are the tasks, responsibilities, risks, and physical demands of this occupation? _____

_____

_____

_____

_____

What skills are required? Put a star beside the skills you already have. _____

_____

_____

_____

_____

What is the work environment like (workload, pace, and people)? How does it look, sound, and smell? _____

_____

_____

_____

_____

What is the work schedule: hours per week, hours per day, overtime expected, travel?

_____

_____

_____

_____

EXPLORING CAREER OPTIONS

What training, education, or other qualifications (licenses, registration, certification) do you need for the occupation? _____

_____

_____

_____

_____

What are the earnings or salary range? _____

_____

_____

_____

What is the employment outlook for this occupation? _____

_____

_____

_____

_____

What are the possibilities for advancement or promotion? _____

_____

_____

_____

_____

What are some related occupations? _____

_____

_____

_____

_____

What are some sources of additional information (books, schools, people)? _____

_____

_____

_____

Networking

Exploring career possibilities is simply a matter of making connections (or *networking*) with people and information. Statistically, networking is the best way to find a job. And there's nothing difficult about it. You already know many people. The people you know also know many people. These folks are all part of your network. Use your network to find out about different occupations and to develop leads on interesting career options. Start with your family; then go to your friends. Don't forget to ask former or current teachers or employers for help. Also talk with people you've met while volunteering in community activities or school organizations. Do they know someone who could help you explore other career areas? (Many people you ask will tell you they don't know anyone who could help you—they're thinking only in terms of someone who could actually give you a job. Remind them that one of their contacts could put you in touch with someone else who could help you.)

It is important to:

▼ Expand your network

▼ Keep track of the people you have contacted and when you talked to them

▼ Write down, in an organized way, the information you get

Expand your network by adding names and phone numbers of people you meet while exploring careers. When you talk with someone about career options, ask if he or she can recommend others who might help you. Ask the people you know for the names and phone numbers of three people they know who might be able to help you. When you contact those people, ask them for the names and numbers of three more people. Very quickly you will have a large network that can help you find the information you want.

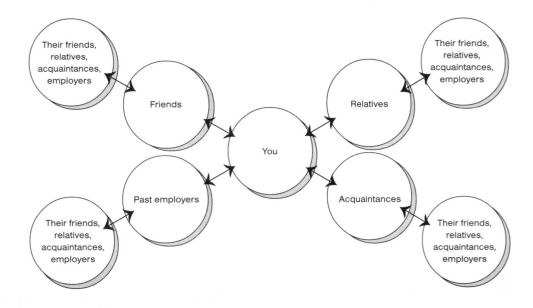

Who You Know

When you network with people, you should collect business cards, flyers, and brochures from people and businesses that interest you. You can store these materials in your portfolio.

Once you have made a decision on your career direction, you can get back in touch with your network for more help. Ask the people in your network to help you find a position. After you are hired, make sure you let the people in your network know about your situation and thank them for all their assistance. The chart below will help you think of your network in a structured way. Add more pages as you need them. Remember to include people from any organizations, teams, or clubs you belong to.

Who I Know

Fill in the information about your own network. Remember, these people can help you discover career options now, and help you find a job later.

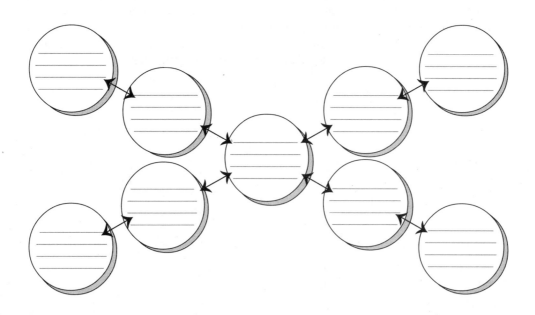

Exploring Your Career Options Checklist

Rate how much you know about exploring career options by completing the checklist below. To further explore your career options, see the resources listed at the end of this section.

Exploring My Career Options Checklist

Put a check mark by the statements that apply to you.

_____ I can identify what would make an ideal job for me.

_____ I can identify a variety of job opportunities available to me with my current skills.

_____ I can identify a variety of job opportunities available to me with some additional training, education, or work experience.

_____ I can identify community resources that support education and training.

_____ I can identify and use information resources that give me details about occupations.

_____ I can identify my network.

Useful ideas to remember in exploring careers: _____

_____

_____

_____

_____

_____

EXPLORING CAREER OPTIONS

Your Journal Entry

Exploring career options involves looking at various occupations and weighing the positives and negatives against your own values and what is most important to you. We all make compromises based on our choices. But you can choose to fulfill short-term goals in order to reach your long-term ones. To that extent, you have the ability to define your future. The exercise below will help you define what is really important to you.

My Journal Entry

In the space provided, write down what you would do if money was not a consideration. Would you go to school? Travel? Work? Would you learn a new skill? Take up a hobby? Invest your money or give it away? Would your goals change after five years? Why or why not?

_____

_____

_____

_____

_____

_____

_____

_____

_____

_____

_____

List of Resources

Assessment Devices

Farr, J. Michael. *The Guide for Occupational Exploration Inventory*. Indianapolis: JIST Works.

Harrington, Thomas F., and Arthur J. O'Shea. *Career Decision-Making System*, Revised. Circle Pines, MN: American Guidance Service.

Liptak, John J. *The Career Exploration Inventory*. Indianapolis: JIST Works.

Associations

American Association of Franchisees and Dealers (AAFD), P.O. Box 81887, San Diego, CA 92138-1887. 619/209-3775. http://www.aafd.org

American Franchisee Association (AFA), 53 West Jackson Boulevard, Suite 205, Chicago, IL 60604. 800/334-4AFA.

Chamber of Commerce of the United States, 1615 H Street NW, Washington, DC 20062. 202/659-6000. http://www.uschamber.org

National Association of Negro Business and Professional Women's Clubs, 1806 New Hampshire Avenue NW, Washington, DC 20009. 202/483-4206. http://www.afrika.com.nanbpwc

National Association of Women Business Owners (NAWBO), 1100 Wayne Avenue, Suite 830, Silver Spring, MD 20910. 301/608-2590. http://www.nawbo.org

U.S. Department of Education, 600 Independence Avenue SW, Washington, DC 20202. 202/401-2000. http://www.ed.gov

U.S. Small Business Administration (SBA), 1110 Vermont Avenue NW, Washington, DC 20005. 800/8ASK-SBA. http://www.sba.gov

Books

Bolles, Richard Nelson. *How to Create a Picture of Your Ideal Job or Next Career*. Berkeley, CA: Ten Speed Press.

The Enhanced Guide to Occupational Information, Second Edition. Indianapolis: JIST Works.

Farr, J. Michael. *The Very Quick Job Search: Get a Better Job in Half the Time, Second Edition.* Indianapolis: JIST Works.

Gilkerson, Linda, and Theresia Paauwe. *Self-Employment: From Dream to Reality!* Indianapolis: JIST Works.

Occupational Outlook Handbook. Indianapolis: JIST Works.

Opportunities in...Series. Lincolnwood, IL: VGM Career Books.

RoAne, Susan. *The Secrets of Savvy Networking: How to Make the Best Connections for Business and Personal Success.* New York: Warner.

Tullier, Michelle. *Networking for Everyone.* Indianapolis: JIST Works.

VGM Professional Careers Series, Lincolnwood, IL: VGM Career Books.

Wolfinger, Anne. *The Quick Internet Guide to Career and Education Information.* Indianapolis: JIST Works.

Young Person's Occupational Outlook Handbook. Indianapolis: JIST Works.

Software

America's Top Jobs™ on CD-ROM! Indianapolis: JIST Works.

CareerMate. W. Newton, MA: The Renascence Company.

Dansky, Howard, and Jeffrey A. Harris. *Vocational Research Institute Inventory.* Philadelphia: Jewish Employment and Vocational Service.

Pinson, Linda, and Jerry Jinnette. *Automate Your Business Plan.* Tustin, CA: Analytical Software Partners & Out of Your Mind...and into the Marketplace™.

Teal, Jack D., and Daryl Hartwig. *Career Compass™.* Bloomington, IL: Meridian.

Part 4

GETTING THERE FROM HERE

By now you've looked at who you are and what you can do. You've also begun exploring careers and thinking about what you'd like to do in the future. But how do you get there from where you are now? In this section, you'll look at your training and education options.

Maybe college is in your plans; you might be thinking of a two- or four-year degree, a master's, or even a Ph.D. or a professional degree. Or perhaps you're thinking of attending a trade or technical school. The military offers training for many careers, and serving in the military is one way to earn scholarship money for a degree program. Some businesses offer on-the-job training. And for some fields, serving an apprenticeship is your foot in the door. The choices may seem overwhelming, but by the time you've finished this section, you'll have a better idea of what kind of training you need and how to get it.

Finally, you'll look at financing your training. Don't discount a career simply because it requires more education than you think you can afford. There are many ways to get the training you need, and in this section you'll learn how to find the resources available to help you on the road to employment.

Does an Education Pay Off?

So far you have looked at your interests, values, and skills, and you've begun exploring which careers fit your own individual mix. But there's another piece to the puzzle in choosing a career, and it's a big one: How much money do you want to make?

One temptation is to give a high priority to jobs that have high earnings. While selecting an occupation based on earnings has some merit, you should consider other points. It is quite possible to get training in a field projected to have high earnings, only to find out later that the region where you want to live has a scarcity of job openings—and earnings are lower as a result. Perhaps this happened because many individuals entered this field, creating an excess of qualified people. It is also possible that you will hate a job that pays well and later decide to change careers so that you can do something you enjoy.

The Department of Labor data below indicates that the average earnings difference between someone with a four-year college degree and someone with a high school education is more than $15,000 a year—enough to buy a nice car or a month vacation to two to Europe! Over a lifetime, this earnings difference will make an enormous difference in lifestyle.

And there is more. Jobs that require more education or training are projected to grow more rapidly than jobs that do not. Note, however, that many rapidly growing and good-paying jobs do not require a four-year degree. Still, most better-paying jobs will require training beyond high school or substantial work experience.

Table. Average annual earnings by education and training category

Educational Level	Average Annual Earnings	Premium over High School Graduates
First professional degree	$55,111	166%
Doctoral degree	$44,162	113%
Master's degree	$35,559	71%
Bachelor's degree	$35,768	72%
Associate degree	$33,317	61%
On-the-job training or experience	$20,699	

Of course, these numbers don't hold true 100 percent of the time. You may know someone with less than a high school education who makes much more than the average. Conversely, you may know someone with a college degree who makes far less. But, on the average, the more education you have, the more money you make.

How Much Education Do You Need?

Following is a list of the top 250 jobs in the United States, as listed in the *Occupational Outlook Handbook*. These are the jobs that more than 85 percent of the population works in. The table also lists average salary levels and the education and training requirements for these jobs. (For detailed descriptions of any of the jobs listed, check out the *Occupational Outlook Handbook* or the *Young Person's OOH*, both based on data from the U.S. Department of Labor and available from JIST Works.)

Look through the list and put a check mark by the job titles that interest you—even if you don't have the required degree. Consider whether your strengths and skills (the ones you listed in Part 2) match the requirements for the job, and whether the job allows you to use the skills you enjoy, matches your values, and gives you the wage level you need. Remember, now is not the time to discount any job just because of the educational requirements. For now, you're only looking at your preferences.

Remember also that how much you make is only one aspect of job satisfaction. Most social workers don't go into the field expecting to get rich—they want to help people. Working at a job you hate simply because it pays a lot is a recipe for disaster. You are almost guaranteed to fail. Wages are important, obviously, but they don't guarantee success or happiness.

For our purposes here, wage levels are defined this way:

Very Low	Less than $20,000 a year
Low	$21,000 to $25,000 a year
Average	$26,000 to $35,000 a year
High	$36,000 to $45,000 a year
Very High	$46,000 or more a year

Top 250 Jobs in the United States

Job Title	Earnings	Education & Training
Executive, Administrative, & Managerial Occupations		
_____ Accountants & Auditors	Average	Bachelor's
_____ Administrative Services Managers	Average	Associate/Bachelor's
_____ Budget Analysts	High	Bachelor's
_____ Construction & Building Inspectors	Average	High school/Associate
_____ Construction Contractors & Managers	Average	Bachelor's
_____ Cost Estimators	Low	Associate/Bachelor's
_____ Educational Administrators	High	Master's/Doctorate
_____ Employment Interviewers	Low	Bachelor's
_____ Engineering, Science, & Data Processing Managers	High	Master's
_____ Financial Managers	High	Bachelor's
_____ Funeral Directors	Average	Specialized training/Professional degree
_____ General Managers & Top Executives	Very High	Bachelor's/Master's/Professional degree
_____ Government Chief Executives & Legislators	High	Bachelor's
_____ Health Services Managers	High	Bachelor's/Master's
_____ Hotel Managers & Assistants	Low	Specialized training/Bachelor's
_____ Industrial Production Managers	Very High	Bachelor's/Professional degree
_____ Inspectors & Compliance Officers, except Construction	Average	Specialized training/Bachelor's
_____ Loan Officers & Counselors	Average	Bachelor's
_____ Management Analysts & Consultants	High	Master's
_____ Marketing, Advertising, & Public Relations Managers	High	Bachelor's
_____ Personnel, Training, & Labor Relations Specialists & Managers	High	Bachelor's
_____ Property & Real Estate Managers	Low	Bachelor's
_____ Purchasers & Buyers	Average	Bachelor's
_____ Restaurant & Food Service Managers	Low	Associate/Bachelor's
_____ Retail Managers	Low	Associate/Bachelor's
_____ Underwriters	Average	Bachelor's
Professional Specialty Occupations		
_____ Engineers	Average to Very High	Bachelor's
_____ Architects	High	Professional degree
_____ Landscape Architects	High	Bachelor's
_____ Surveyors	Average	Bachelor's
_____ Actuaries	Average	Bachelor's
_____ Computer Scientists & Systems Analysts	High	Bachelor's
_____ Mathematicians	Average	Bachelor's
_____ Operations Research Analysts	High	Master's
_____ Statisticians	High	Bachelor's
_____ Scientists	Average to Very High	Bachelor's/Master's/Doctoral
_____ Lawyers & Judges	Very High	Professional degree
_____ Social Scientists & Urban Planners	High to Very High	Master's/Doctorate

Job Title	Earnings	Education & Training
_____ Economists & Marketing Research Analysts	High	Bachelor's
_____ Psychologists	Very High	Doctorate
_____ Sociologists	High	Master's
_____ Urban & Regional Planners	Average	Bachelor's/Masters
_____ Human Services Workers	Very Low to Low	High school/Bachelor's
_____ Recreation Workers	Low	High school/Bachelor's
_____ Social Workers	Average	Bachelor's/Master's
_____ Clergy	Average	Bachelor's/Professional degree
_____ Teachers	Average	Bachelor's/Master's
_____ Archivists & Curators	Average	Master's/Doctorate
_____ College & University Faculty	High	Doctorate
_____ Counselors	Average	Master's
_____ Librarians	Average	Professional degree
_____ Medical Practitioners	Very High	Professional degree
_____ Veterinarians	Very High	Professional degree
_____ Dietitians & Nutritionists	Average	Bachelor's
_____ Occupational Therapists	High	Bachelor's
_____ Pharmacists	High	Professional degree
_____ Physical Therapists	Average	Bachelor's
_____ Physician Assistants	High	Bachelor's
_____ Recreational Therapists	Average	Associate/Bachelor's
_____ Registered Nurses	Average	Bachelor's/Professional degree
_____ Respiratory Therapists	Average	Associate
_____ Speech-Language Pathologists & Audiologists	High	Master's
_____ Public Relations Specialists	Average	Bachelor's
_____ Radio & TV Announcers & Newscasters	Very Low to Average	Specialized training/Bachelor's
_____ Reporters & Correspondents	Average	Bachelor's
_____ Writers & Editors	Low to Average	Bachelor's
_____ Designers	Average	Associate/Bachelor's
_____ Photographers & Camera Operators	Low	Specialized training/Bachelor's
_____ Visual Artists	Low	Specialized training/Bachelor's
_____ Actors, Directors, & Producers	Very Low to Very High	Specialized training/Bachelor's
_____ Dancers & Choreographers	Average	Specialized training
_____ Musicians	Very Low to Very High	Specialized training/Bachelor's

Technicians & Related Support Occupations

_____ Medical Technologists & Technicians	Low to Average	Associate/Bachelor's/ Specialized training
_____ Aircraft Pilots	Very High	Associate/Bachelor's/ Specialized training
_____ Air Traffic Controllers	Very High	Bachelor's/Specialized training
_____ Broadcast Technicians	Very Low to Low	Associate/Bachelor's
_____ Computer Programmers	Average to High	Bachelor's
_____ Drafters	Average	Associate
_____ Engineering Technicians	Low	Associate
_____ Library Technicians	Low	High School/Associate/Bachelor's
_____ Paralegals	Average	Associate/Bachelor's
_____ Science Technicians	Low to Average	Associate/Bachelor's

Marketing & Sales Occupations

_____ Sales Workers	Very Low	High School
_____ Sales Agents	Average to Very High	Bachelor's/Specialized training
_____ Travel Agents	Very Low to Low	Specialized training

Job Title	Earnings	Education & Training
Administrative Support Occupations, Including Clerical		
_____ Adjusters, Investigators, & Collectors	Low	Bachelor's/Specialized training
_____ Bank Tellers	Very Low	High School/Specialized training
_____ Clerical Supervisors & Managers	Average	Associate/Bachelor's
_____ Computer & Peripheral Equipment Operators	Low to Average	Bachelor's
_____ Clerks	Very Low to Low	High School/Specialized training
_____ Mail Clerks & Messengers	Very Low	High School
_____ Material Recording, Scheduling, Dispatching, & Distributing Workers	Very Low	High School
_____ Dispatchers	Low	High School
_____ Postal Clerks & Mail Carriers	Average	High School
_____ Library Assistants & Bookmobile Drivers	Very Low	High School
_____ Secretaries	Low	High School/Associate
_____ Stenographers & Court Reporters	Low	Specialized training
_____ Teacher Aides	Very Low	High School/Associate
_____ Telephone Operators	Low	High School/Specialized training
_____ Typists, Word Processors, & Data Entry Keyers	Very Low	High School
Service Occupations		
_____ Correction Officers	Average	High School/Specialized training
_____ Fire Fighters	Average	High School/Specialized training
_____ Guards	Very Low	High School
_____ Police, Detectives, & Special Agents	Average	Bachelor's/Specialized training
_____ Chefs, Cooks, & Other Kitchen Service Workers	Very Low	High School
_____ Food & Beverage Service Workers	Very Low	High School
_____ Medical Assistants	Very Low	High School/Specialized training
_____ Animal Caretakers, except Farm	Very Low	High School/Specialized training
_____ Barbers & Cosmetologists	Very Low	High School/Specialized training
_____ Preschool Workers	Very Low to Low	High School/Associate
_____ Flight Attendants	Very Low to Low	Bachelor's/Specialized training
_____ Gardeners & Groundskeepers	Very Low	High School/Specialized training
_____ Homemaker-Home Health Aides	Very Low	High School
_____ Janitors, Cleaners, & Cleaning Supervisors	Very Low	High School
_____ Private Household Workers	Very Low	High School
Agriculture, Forestry, Fishing, & Related Occupations		
_____ Farm Operators & Managers	Very Low to Average	Bachelor's/Specialized training
_____ Fishers, Hunters, & Trappers	Average	Specialized training
_____ Forestry & Logging Workers	Very Low	Specialized training
Mechanics, Installers, & Repairers		
_____ Mechanics	Very Low to Average	High School/Associate/ Specialized training
_____ Equipment Repairers	Low to Average	High School/Associate/ Specialized Training
_____ Line Installers & Cable Splicers	Average	High School/Specialized Training
_____ Millwrights	Average	High School/Specialized Training
_____ Musical Instrument Repairers & Tuners	Average	Specialized training
Construction Trades & Extractive Occupations		
_____ Bricklayers & Stonemasons	Low	High School/Specialized training
_____ Carpenters	Low	High School/Specialized training

Job Title	Earnings	Education & Training
_____ Carpet Installers	Low	Specialized training
_____ Concrete Masons & Terrazzo Workers	Low	High School/Specialized training
_____ Drywall Workers & Lathers	Low	Specialized training
_____ Electricians	Average	High School/Specialized training
_____ Glaziers	Low	High School/Specialized training
_____ Insulation Workers	Low	Specialized training
_____ Painters & Paperhangers	Very Low	Specialized training
_____ Plasterers	Low	High School/Specialized training
_____ Plumbers & Pipefitters	Average	High School/Specialized training
_____ Roofers	Low	High School/Specialized training
_____ Roustabouts	Average	High School/Specialized training
_____ Sheetmetal Workers	Average	High School/Specialized training
_____ Structural & Reinforcing Ironworkers	Low	High School/Specialized training
_____ Tilesetters	Low	High School/Specialized training

Production Occupations

Job Title	Earnings	Education & Training
_____ Precision Assemblers	Very Low	High School/Specialized training
_____ Blue-Collar Worker Supervisors	Average	High School/Specialized training
_____ Butchers & Meat, Poultry, & Fish Cutters	Low	Specialized training
_____ Inspectors, Testers, & Graders	Low	High School/Specialized training
_____ Boilermakers	Average	High School/Specialized training
_____ Jewelers	Low to Average	High school/Specialized training
_____ Machinists & Tool Programmers	Average	High School/Specialized training
_____ Machinery Operators	Very Low to Low	High School/Specialized training
_____ Tool & Die Makers	Average	Associate/Specialized training
_____ Welders, Cutters, & Welding Machine Operators	Low	High School/Specialized training
_____ Electronic Power Generating Plant Operators & Power Distributors & Dispatchers	High	High School/Specialized training
_____ Stationary Engineers	Average	High School/Specialized training
_____ Water & Wastewater Treatment Plant Operators	Average	Associate/Specialized training
_____ Prepress Workers	Average	High School/Specialized training
_____ Bindery Workers	Very Low	High School/Specialized training
_____ Apparel Workers	Very Low	Specialized training
_____ Shoe & Leather Workers & Repairers	Low	Specialized training
_____ Upholsterers	Very Low	Specialized training
_____ Woodworkers	Very Low	High School/Specialized training
_____ Dental Laboratory Technicians	Average	Associate/Specialized training
_____ Ophthalmic Laboratory Technicians	Very Low	High School/Specialized training
_____ Photographic Process Workers	Very Low	High School/Specialized training

Transportation & Material Moving Occupations

Job Title	Earnings	Education & Training
_____ Bus Drivers	Low	High School
_____ Material Moving Equipment Operators	Low	High School/Specialized training
_____ Rail Transportation Workers	Average	High School/Specialized training
_____ Taxi Drivers & Chauffeurs	Very Low	Specialized training
_____ Truck Drivers	Low	High School/Specialized training
_____ Water Transportation Workers	Very Low to High	High School/Bachelor's
_____ Handlers, Equipment Cleaners, Helpers, & Laborers	Very Low	High School
_____ Armed Forces Jobs	Average	High School

GETTING THERE FROM HERE

Go to the Experts

One good way to find out what kind of training you need is to ask someone who works in the job that interests you. Chances are, someone in your community is employed in the kind of job you want, and most people love to talk about themselves and their work. So your next step in planning your education is to talk with the experts. Ask your parents, your teachers, your counselor, and your friends if they know anyone who does the kind of work you're interested in. Then call that person and ask if he or she will either meet with you in person or talk with you on the phone.

Another idea is to call the person who supervises people in the job you like. This gives you some insight into what managers look for in the people they hire for the job. In either case, ask these questions and record your answers below. (Make copies of this page if you plan to make more than one call.)

What is the education level of most people in this job? _____

_____

What kind of training do I need to do this job? _____

_____

Do I need a high school, associate, bachelor's, or advanced degree? _____

_____

Is there a specific college major I should pursue? _____

Do I need specialized training? _____

Is that training provided on the job, or will I have to complete a training program before I

can be hired? _____

Where did you receive your training? _____

Are there any schools or training institutes that are well known in this field for producing

good workers? _____

Are there any professional associations or unions I should contact for more information?

_____

Checking Out Your Options

By now you should have a good idea of what kind of training or education you need to do the job you want. But where are you going to get that training? You have several options, which are detailed below. Check those you are interested in pursuing. Use your school counseling office, the library, or a local community college to find out what training programs are offered in your area. Some of these options are explored in more detail in the following pages.

✔ I could get more training by...	Where	When
❑ Reading journals or books to update my knowledge		
❑ Taking some courses or workshops		
❑ Enrolling in a trade, technical, or vocational school		
❑ Enrolling in a two-year program		
❑ Enrolling in a four-year program		
❑ Joining the military service		
❑ Beginning an apprenticeship program		
❑ Beginning a job-training program		
❑ Taking a temporary job that would add to my skills		
❑ Other		

84

GETTING THERE FROM HERE

On-the-Job Training

You could go straight from high school to work, and let your employer train you to do your job. The main advantages to this approach are that you begin to earn money immediately, and you have no debt during your training. Some companies have extensive training programs for new employees, involving classroom instruction and hands-on work. Some will even pay you while you train, while others have you go through a training program first and then take a test to qualify for a paid position.

On-the-job training has at least two possible disadvantages. First, you typically learn about only one job, which means you have less job mobility. Second, many jobs that require no education beyond high school pay lower wages and offer little room for advancement.

Jobs that require only on-the-job training include retail sales, clerical, janitorial and housekeeping, food and beverage serving, painting and wallpapering, and some construction work.

To find out about on-the-job training opportunities, contact organizations in your area directly and ask if they provide training programs. Be sure you get answers to these questions:

Am I guaranteed a job once I have completed the program? _____

_____

What will my training qualify me to do? _____

_____

Will I receive some kind of certification when I have completed the training? _____

_____

Will there be opportunities for further training and job mobility later?_____

_____

What courses should I be taking in high school to prepare for the job? _____

_____

Apprenticeships

Apprenticeships are similar to on-the-job training programs because you learn while you work, usually under the close supervision of a skilled journey worker. Apprenticeships also include some related technical instruction in a classroom.

With about 1,000 hours allocated for each six-month period, apprenticeship programs range from 2,000 to 12,000 hours of training, depending on the occupation and the standards recognized by the industry, but typically last 8,000 hours, or four years. Those hours include a minimum of 144 hours per year for classroom instruction. At the end of the training period, an apprentice receives a Certificate of Completion of Apprenticeship from the U.S. Department of Labor, Bureau of Apprenticeship and Training (BAT).

To be considered for an apprenticeship, an individual must have a high school diploma (or a General Education Development Test Certificate) and be physically able to perform the work of the trade. The minimum allowable age is 16, but 18 is usually the age set for entry into a registered program.

Apprenticeships offer you a chance to earn while you learn and are a good entry point to many careers. Usually, an apprentice's pay begins at about half that of an experienced worker and periodically increases during the apprenticeship.

Apprenticeships offer versatility because they teach all aspects of a trade. Compared to other on-the-job training, apprenticeships offer more job mobility because you can take your certification elsewhere. Employers value more highly the training received in registered programs. Craftworkers who were apprentices tend to be better workers and are more likely to become supervisors than those who had only informal training.

About 100,000 individuals become apprentices each year. At any given time during a year, about 350,000 persons are in 43,000 registered programs. When economic conditions are good, more skilled workers are needed, and more apprentices must be trained to meet the need, especially in construction and industrial production. When economic conditions are bad, the need for apprentices lessens.

Most apprentices work in the building trades—especially as electricians, carpenters, and plumbers—or in industry as pipe fitters and sheet metal workers. Apprenticeships are offered also in tool and die making, machining, and welding, and in some public service occupations, such as fire fighting, law enforcement, and emergency medical care.

To find out about apprenticeships, contact your local office of the Bureau of Apprenticeship and Training. It's listed in the phone directory under United States Government—Department of Labor.

Be sure to ask some specific questions before you begin an apprenticeship:

How long will the apprenticeship last? _____

_____

Will I work full-time during the apprenticeship? _____

What wage will I receive during my apprenticeship? _____

How much time will I spend in the classroom, and how much will I spend on the job?

_____

Do I have to supply my own tools? What tools will I need? _____

_____

What are my chances of getting a job in the field *in my area* at the end of the apprentice-

ship? _____

_____

Will I be certified as a journey worker at the end of the apprenticeship? _____

_____

Trade or Technical School

A trade or technical school allows you to take extensive coursework in just the field you're studying. Most programs can be completed in just two years, which means you can enter the job market that much sooner. Technical institutes often employ industry professionals to teach their courses, which means you get the opportunity to learn from people working in the field. They also usually have extensive career services.

Some fields for which you can prepare at a technical institute are medical technology, engineering technology, dental hygiene, paralegal work, and graphic design.

Tuition is relatively inexpensive but can vary, depending on the length of the program and the type of equipment used. For example, programs in aircraft mechanics and maintenance and computer-aided drafting are likely to cost more than programs in accounting.

Trade schools are the only places to learn some professions. If you want to become a barber, cosmetologist, bartender, flight attendant, or truck driver, for example, a trade school is the place to do it. Most are less expensive than two- and four-year degrees, and you focus on only one field.

If you are interested in certain fields, trade schools may be the way to go. Just be sure to investigate the one you're looking at carefully. Be sure it is accredited by the Accrediting Commission of Career Schools & Colleges of Technology, and check with your local Chamber of Commerce or Better Business Bureau to find out about complaints.

Trade and technical schools offer a direct route to certain careers, but you must do your homework to find the best. Be sure to get these questions answered, before you sign any agreements:

Is the school accredited by the Accrediting Commission of Career Schools & Colleges of Technology? _____

Is financial aid available to students? _____

_____

What is the cost of tuition, and how much does it increase from year to year? _____

_____

What is the placement rate for graduates? _____

_____

_____

Does the school offer job search services? _____

_____

Can the school provide a list of companies for which graduates work? _____

_____

Associate Degree

An associate degree can be earned at a community or junior college or from a traditional four-year college and typically takes two years of full-time study. Associate degrees are roughly equivalent to completing the freshman and sophomore years of college, but they are often connected directly to an occupation. Department of Labor statistics show that workers with associate degrees average $5,000 a year more than high school graduates in salary. And if you decide to go on to a four-year degree program, an associate degree usually can be applied toward your bachelor's degree.

Because you can earn an associate degree at community colleges, some people consider them the best bargains in education. Community colleges tend to be less expensive than traditional colleges and universities, and most students attending them live off-campus or at home, which lowers the cost as well.

An associate degree prepares you for many kinds of jobs, including retail or restaurant manager, medical technician, legal secretary, preschool teacher, computer technician, dental lab technician, and drafter.

You can obtain many good jobs with an associate degree, but many other good jobs require a bachelor's degree.

GETTING THERE FROM HERE

For more information about associate degrees, contact your local community or junior college, or a nearby college or university. Be sure to ask these questions:

Is the school accredited? _____

Is financial aid available? _____

What is the cost of tuition, and how much does it increase from year to year? _____

_____

How long will it take me to earn my associate degree? _____

Will the associate degree I'm considering apply toward a bachelor's degree if I decide to

continue my education? _____

_____

Does the school offer job search assistance? _____

_____

What is the job finding rate for graduates? _____

_____

Bachelor's Degree

This is what most people think of when they talk of a college education. A bachelor's degree usually requires four years of full-time study and can be earned at a college or a university. Earning a bachelor's degree signals to an employer that you have a broad base of knowledge, you can stick with a program, and you have learned how to learn. All of these are marketable skills.

In a traditional four-year program, you will study a broad array of subjects in the first two years, such as English, math, sociology, history, and a foreign language. In the final two years, you will specialize in one field—your major—and that is what your degree shows. You will hold a B.A. (Bachelor of Arts) *in* English, or a B.S. (Bachelor of Science) *in* Psychology, *in* Business, etc.

A college education at public universities averages $8,990 for tuition, room and board, books and supplies, and transportation. The total average cost for a year at a private four-year school is $18,784. The good news is that there are more ways than ever to finance an education, and in the next section, we'll look at some of those.

College graduates earn an average of $35,768 a year—about 72 percent more than the average high school graduate does and $10,000 more than the average for all workers. The earnings of those who start a college program but don't graduate, however, are often lower than those of two-year graduates. While it is probably a good idea to think about potential earnings when you choose a college education, it is only one thing to consider. Being satisfied with your work—and your life—can be even more important than how much you earn.

Some of the careers for which a bachelor's degree prepares you are accountant, management analyst, underwriter, engineer, computer scientist, meteorologist, teacher, occupational or physical therapist, registered nurse, public relations specialist, reporter, editor, and computer programmer.

For more information on earning a bachelor's degree, check with your counselor's office or a local college or university. Look at your library for one of the several guides to colleges, which offer comparisons based on cost, student life, academic standards, accreditation, credit transfers, and just about anything else you can think of.

If you're looking at investing thousands of dollars and four years of your life in earning a degree, there are some questions you should ask of the school:

Is the school accredited? By whom? _____

What is the attrition rate (the drop-out rate)? _____

_____

What percentage of the student body graduates within four years? How many students

take longer? _____

_____

Will I be required to live on campus? _____

_____

Does the school offer job search assistance? _____

_____

What is the total cost for tuition, books and supplies, and room and board? _____

_____

How much do those costs increase yearly? _____

_____

What percentage of the student body receives financial aid? _____

_____

When are the deadlines for applying for admission and financial aid? _____

_____

What courses should I be taking in high school to prepare for college? _____

_____

Military Training

Despite recent cutbacks, the U.S. military is still the nation's largest employer. About 200,000 young men and women join the military each year, and for many, it provides a sure route to education and a good career. Some people decide to stay in the military and make it a career, but many others take advantage of the training they receive in the military to find civilian jobs when their service is ended. The military trains people to work in hospitals, repair and fly aircraft, program computers, operate nuclear facilities, and acquire a host of other skills that are directly applicable to civilian jobs. Military service also can be the way to finance a college education.

Military life is much more regimented than civilian life, and you must be willing to accept this. Remember that signing an enlistment contract obligates you to serve for a specified period. In the event of war, many military personnel may engage in combat.

The important thing is to make an informed decision. Don't assume it's your only way to get an education. Talk with your local service recruiter, ask all the questions you may have, and then take some time to think over your choices. Talk with family and friends. If you can, find people who have served in the military and talk with them about their experiences.

Finally, if you want to pursue military service, you will have to take the Armed Services Vocational Aptitude Battery (ASVAB). The military uses the ASVAB to identify which jobs in the military will match your skills and talents. Ask at your school's career center or at your local recruiter's office for the ASVAB Information Pamphlet, which will tell you more about the test and give you some sample questions.

Each of the military services publishes handbooks, fact sheets, and pamphlets describing entrance requirements, training and advancement opportunities, and other aspects of military careers. These publications are widely available at all recruiting stations, most state employment service offices, and in high schools, colleges, and public libraries.

GETTING THERE FROM HERE

When you talk with your service recruiter, be sure to get answers to these questions:

If I sign up, how long must I stay in the military? _____

Do I get any choice in where I am stationed? _____

Where am I most likely to be stationed? _____
_____

What is my base pay? _____

What jobs in the military do my ASVAB scores qualify me for? _____
_____

What are my chances of getting trained in the job I want? _____
_____

Are there any other tests I must pass in order to get the job I want? _____
_____

Checking Out Schools

Some people know, right from the start, where they will get their education or training. But, if you're like most people, you have more than one option you're looking at. In that case, it's a good idea to take your time about making any decisions. Talk with the admissions people at all the schools or programs you're considering; then fill in the information you receive on the following form. (Make extra copies of this form if needed.) Keep these ideas in mind as you gather your information:

▼ **Get the employer's viewpoint.** Employers sometimes recruit from certain training programs and not others. If you are considering more education or training for a particular career, talk with employers before you enroll. Ask them what they think of the program and if they prefer to hire from a specific program.

▼ **Do some comparison shopping.** Just as tuition and fees vary from one school to another, so does training. Call a number of programs to compare the quality and cost. Consider the time of day classes are held, the length of the program, if you can get credit for work experience, and whether you can take courses by correspondence or alternative ways.

▼ **Find out about accreditation.** Most schools (public or private, college or university, trade or technical) are certified by a national organization. This group determines if the program offers good-quality training. Ask if the school is accredited and by what organization? If in doubt, your state department of education will either know the answer or refer you to someone who does.

▼ **Ask about financial aid or tuition assistance.** Don't rule out more training or education because of financial reasons. Most schools have financial aid programs. Special programs in your area may provide funds for training. Find out if you qualify. If you are currently working, your place of employment may help you get training or further education by paying all or part of the costs. Check it out.

Checking Out Schools Worksheet

School: _____

City: _____ State: _____

Expenses per year: _____

_____

Accreditation by: _____

_____

_____

Program requirements: _____

_____

_____

_____

Notes: _____

_____

_____

_____

_____

_____

_____

_____

_____

_____

_____

_____

Checking Out Schools Worksheet

School: _____

City: _____ State: _____

Expenses per year: _____

_____

Accreditation by: _____

_____

_____

Program requirements: _____

_____

_____

_____

Notes: _____

_____

_____

_____

_____

_____

_____

_____

_____

_____

_____

_____

_____

Checking Out Schools Worksheet

School: _____

City: _____ State: _____

Expenses per year: _____
_____

Accreditation by: _____
_____
_____

Program requirements: _____
_____
_____
_____

Notes: _____
_____
_____
_____
_____
_____
_____
_____
_____
_____
_____
_____
_____

Checking Out Schools Worksheet

School: _____

City: _____ State: _____

Expenses per year: _____

_____

Accreditation by: _____

_____

_____

Program requirements: _____

_____

_____

_____

Notes: _____

_____

_____

_____

_____

_____

_____

_____

_____

_____

_____

_____

_____

_____

Getting Financial Aid

As you saw earlier, the cost of an education may seem huge. But consider this: Nearly half of all college, technical, and trade school students in the United States receive financial aid. There are ways to get the money you need for your education. In this section, we'll look at the different sources of financial aid and how to apply for them.

The federal government uses a standard formula to determine whether you qualify for financial assistance. Basically, you list the total cost for a year of school, including tuition and fees, books and supplies, housing and meals, transportation, and personal expenses. Then you list your own income (during the summer and during the school year); your savings; and your family's income, savings, and assets. The government has a set formula for determining what percentage of your and your family's income, assets, and savings to use. They then deduct that amount from the estimated cost of the school to determine your need, like this:

    Estimated cost
    –Estimated resources
    _____
    Estimated need

My Costs and Resources Worksheet

Before you talk to the financial aid counselor at the school you're considering, gather together all your information here.

Estimated Costs

Direct Costs

Tuition and fees: _____

Books and supplies: _____

Indirect Costs

Housing*: _____

Meals*: _____

Transportation: _____

Personal expenses: _____

Total Estimated Cost: _____

Many schools offer a single room-and-board plan, but some offer several different alternatives. Ask about the cost at the school you're considering.

Estimated Resources

My Resources:

Summer income: _____

Income during school year: _____

My savings and assets: _____

My Family's Resources:

My parents' income: _____

My parents' savings: _____

My parents' assets (including the family home): _____

Sources of Financial Aid

The financial aid counselor at the school you're considering will be happy to talk with you about programs offered by the federal government, your state, and the school. But here is a brief look at the major government programs:

Federal Pell Grants do not have to be repaid when you finish school. They are awarded based on need to students pursuing their first undergraduate degree. To apply, you must submit the Free Application for Federal Student Aid (available from the college's financial aid office or your state student assistance office). You should submit your application—as soon after January 1 as possible—to the address on the form.

Federal Supplementary Education Opportunity Grants also do not have to be repaid. They are awarded to students with great financial need. Ask for information about these grants and the deadlines for application at the financial aid office of the school you are considering.

Federal Perkins Loans are made by colleges to their students and must be repaid when the student graduates or leaves school. They are based on need. The loans have a low, fixed interest rate, and the student pays no interest while in school. The money comes from the government, but the school makes the decision about who gets the loans. Ask at the financial aid office of the school you are considering.

Federal Stafford Loans are made by banks, credit unions, and savings and loan associations, and are guaranteed by the government. Call the Federal Student Aid Information Center at 800/433-3243 for information about these loans. They will direct you to your state guaranty agency. If you qualify for a subsidized loan (based on need), the government pays the interest on your loan while you are in school. Otherwise, you will be charged interest on your loan from the day you receive the money.

Federal Direct Student Loans are made by the U.S. Department of Education and processed through colleges and universities. Ask at your prospective school's financial aid office for more information.

The Federal Work-Study Program allows students to work at jobs at their school or at a nonprofit organization, with their salary going to offset the cost of their education. In effect, you work at a job, and the government pays the school 75 percent of your salary. This is a need-based program. Ask for information at your school's financial aid office.

State Programs

All 50 states offer some kind of financial aid based on need. Many also offer merit scholarships to students who stay in-state for school. Some offer subsidized loans to students. Call your state's department of higher education for information about your state's programs.

Setting Your Schedule for Success

Your Junior Year

Use the worksheet below to record the courses you take that will prepare you for your chosen career:

First Semester:

_____

_____

_____

_____

_____

_____

_____

Second Semester:

_____

_____

_____

_____

_____

_____

_____

Junior Year Timeline

Use the checklist here to record deadlines and dates. Check the items off as you complete them.

Date Due   **Done**

_____ _____ Talk with your guidance counselor about career information.

_____ _____ Begin information interviews with people employed in jobs that interest me.

_____ _____ Sign up for the PSAT test if I'm planning on continuing my education.

_____ _____ Begin writing to colleges, technical institutes, or trade schools for information and catalogs.

_____ _____ Join a job club or take a part-time job that will help prepare me for my chosen field.

_____ _____ Attend college or job fairs in my community.

_____ _____ Visit nearby colleges, technical institutes, or trade schools; schedule advance meetings with admissions and financial aid officers.

_____ _____ Look through school catalogs for information about admissions tests and deadlines.

_____ _____ Take the ACT or SAT in the spring, as practice.

Your Senior Year

Use the worksheet below to record the courses you take that will prepare you for your chosen career:

First Semester:

_____

_____

_____

_____

_____

_____

_____

_____

Second Semester:

_____

_____

_____

_____

_____

_____

_____

_____

Senior Year Timeline

Use the timeline here to check off deadlines and dates:

**Date
Due**   **Done**

_____   _____   Meet with your guidance counselor to make sure you are on schedule to graduate.

_____   _____   Sign up for any courses you must have to graduate.

_____   _____   Take the ACT or SAT if you didn't take it last year.

_____   _____   Visit schools that interest you.

_____   _____   Attend job and college fairs.

_____   _____   Narrow your choices to three or four schools.

_____   _____   Write down deadlines for admissions and financial aid applications for those schools.

_____   _____   Meet with your school counselor to discuss your education choices and financial aid.

_____   _____   Arrange for teachers to write letters of recommendation; ask for copies to keep in your portfolio.

_____   _____   Complete and mail all admissions forms by deadlines (keep copies).

_____   _____   Complete and mail all financial aid applications by deadlines (keep copies).

_____   _____   Graduate—and start a whole new adventure!

GETTING THERE FROM HERE

Getting Your Training Checklist

In today's competitive job market, it's more important than ever to get the right training for your career. You've looked at your options for getting that training. Check now to see what you've learned.

Getting My Training Checklist

_____ I know what kind of education or training I need for the career I want.

_____ I can interview people who do the work that interests me, to find out how they got their training.

_____ I know how to investigate possible sources of training.

_____ I know the pros and cons of on-the-job training.

_____ I know the pros and cons of apprenticeships.

_____ I know the pros and cons of trade and technical schools.

_____ I know the pros and cons of getting an associate degree.

_____ I know the pros and cons of getting a bachelor's degree.

_____ I know the pros and cons of getting my training in the military.

_____ I understand what the ASVAB is used for.

_____ I have gathered my family's information to apply for financial aid.

_____ I know whom to contact for more information about financial aid.

_____ I have scheduled myself for success in my junior and senior years.

GETTING THERE FROM HERE

Your Journal Entry

Getting the right training and education can mean the difference between success and failure in the job market. Now that you've thought about your education choices, take a few minutes to think about the option you've chosen. Are you satisfied with it? Is it your first choice or a compromise? What might be standing in the way of achieving your first choice? Can you find a way around any obstacles? You owe it to yourself to try.

My Journal Entry

In the space below, describe your planned path to getting the education and training you need. Include any obstacles you foresee and how you plan to get around them.

This is how I plan to get the training I need:

_____

_____

_____

_____

_____

_____

_____

_____

_____

_____

_____

_____

_____

List of Resources

Books

American Association of Community Colleges. *AACC Membership Directory*. Washington, DC: AACC.

American Trade School Directory. Jericho, NY: Croner Publications, Updated monthly.

Andrews, Linda Landis. *How to Choose a College Major*. Lincolnwood, IL: VGM Career Horizons.

Barron's Profiles of American Colleges. Hauppage, NY: Barron's Educational, Updated yearly.

Bear, John, & Mariah Bear. *Bears' Guide to Earning College Degrees Nontraditionally*. Benicia, CA: C&B Publications, Updated yearly.

Beckham, Barry (Ed.). *The Black Student's Guide to Scholarships, 4th Edition: 600+ Private Money Sources for Black and Minority Students*. New York: Madison Books.

Betterton, Don M. *How the Military Will Help You Pay for College, 2nd Edition*. Princeton, NJ: Peterson's Guides.

Brennan, Moya, & Sarah Briggs. *How to Apply to American Colleges & Universities*. Lincolnwood, IL: NTC Publishing Group.

Brownstein, S. C., M. Weiner, & S. Weiner Green. *How to Prepare for the Scholastic Aptitude Test, SAT*. Hauppauge, NY: Barron's Educational.

Butler, Joel. *High-Technology Degree Alternatives: Earning a High-Tech Degree While Working Full Time*. Belmont, CA: Professional Publications.

Career Paths: Guide to Business and Other Internships, Scholarships, and Career Development Opportunities for Minority Students. Washington, DC: National Urban League.

Cassidy, Daniel J. *The Scholarship Book, 5th Edition: The Complete Guide to Private-Sector Scholarships, Grants & Loans for Undergraduates*. Englewood Cliffs, NJ: Prentice-Hall.

Cass-Liepman, Julia. *Cass & Birnbaum's Guide to American Colleges*. New York: HarperCollins, Updated yearly.

Chronicle Vocational School Manual: Guide to Accredited Vocational Schools. Moravia, NY: Chronicle Guidance Publications, Updated yearly.

College Blue Book: Occupational Education. New York: Macmillan, Updated yearly.

College Financial Aid Made Easy for the 1998-99 Academic Year. Berkeley, CA: Ten Speed Press.

College Scholarship Service. *College Costs & Financial Aid Handbook*. New York: College Board Publications, Updated yearly.

Collins, Robert F. *Qualifying for Admission to the Service Academies*. New York: Rosen.

Curris, Joan, with Michael R. Crystal. *SAT Success*. Princeton, NJ: Peterson's Guides.

Davis, Kristen. *Financing College: How to Use Savings, Financial Aid, Scholarships, & Loans to Afford the School of Your Choice*. Washington, DC: Kiplinger.

Dollars for College Series. Garrett Park, MD: Garrett Park Press.

Duffy, James P. *College Online: How to Take College Courses Without Leaving Home*. New York: Wiley.

Encyclopedia of Careers and Vocational Guidance, 9th Edition. Chicago: J. G. Ferguson Publishing.

Financial Aid for Minorities Series. Garrett Park, MD: Garrett Park Press.

Frank, Steven, R. Fred Zuker & the Staff of Kaplan Educational Centers. *The Road to College: Selection, Admissions, Financial Aid*. New York: Simon & Schuster.

Hill, Livern (Ed.). *Black American Colleges & Universities: Profiles of Two-Year, Four-Year & Professional Schools*. Detroit: Gale Research.

Kirby, Debra M. *Fund Your Way Through College: Uncovering 1,700 Great Opportunities in Undergraduate Financial Aid*. Detroit: Visible Ink Press.

Klein, Henry. *College in Your Future: 140 Questions and Answers About Getting In—Staying In*. Garrett Park, MD: Garrett Park Press.

Ludden, LaVerne L. & Marsha Ludden. *Luddens' Adult Guide to Colleges and Universities: A Directory of Thousands of Adult-Friendly Degree Programs*. Indianapolis: Park Avenue.

Ludden, LeVerne L. *Back to School: A College Guide for Adults*. Indianapolis: Park Avenue.

Macmillan Guide to Correspondence Study, 6th Edition. New York: Macmillan.

Maki, Kathleen E. & Kathleen M. Savage (Eds.). *Professional Careers Sourcebook*, 5th Edition: *Where to Find Help Planning Careers That Require College or Technical Degrees*. Detroit: Gale Research.

Maki, Kathleen E. & Kathleen M. Savage (Eds.). *Vocational Careers Sourcebook*, 3rd Edition: *Where to Find Help Planning Careers in Skilled, Trade, and Non-technical Careers*. Detroit: Gale Research.

Martin, Garrett D. & Barbara E. Baker. *National Directory of Internships*. Raleigh, NJ: National Society for Experimental Education.

Mintz, Jerry (Ed.). *The Handbook of Alternative Education*. New York: Macmillan.

Occupational Outlook Handbook. Indianapolis: JIST Works.

Otto, Luther B. *Helping Your Child Choose a Career*. Indianapolis: JIST Works.

Peterson's College Money Handbook. Princeton, NJ: Peterson's Guides, Updated yearly.

Peterson's Guide to Certificate Programs at American Colleges and Universities. Princeton, NJ: Peterson's Guides.

Peterson's Guide to Four-Year Colleges. Princeton, NJ: Peterson's Guides, Updated yearly.

Peterson's Guide to Internships: Over 35,000 Opportunities to Get an Edge in Today's Competitive Job Market. Princeton, NJ: Peterson's Guides, Updated yearly.

Peterson's Guide to Summer Jobs for Students: Where the Jobs Are & How to Get Them. Princeton, NJ: Peterson's Guides, Updated yearly.

Peterson's Guide to Two-Year Colleges. Princeton, NJ: Peterson's Guides, Updated yearly.

Phifer, Paul. *College Majors and Careers: A Resource Guide to Effective Life Planning*. Chicago: J. G. Ferguson.

Princeton Review: The Best 311 Colleges. New York: Random House, Updated yearly.

Roes, Nicholas A. *America's Lowest Cost Colleges*, 8th Edition. Barryville, NJ: NAR Publications.

Rowe, Fred A. *The Career Connection for College Education: A Guide to College Education & Related Career Opportunities.* Indianapolis: JIST Works.

Rowe, Fred A. *The Career Connection for Technical Education: A Guide to Technical Training & Related Career Opportunities.* Indianapolis: JIST Works.

Schwartz, John. *Arco's College Scholarship & Financial Aid.* New York: Macmillan.

Solórzano, Lucia. *Barron's Best Buys in College Education,* 4th Edition. Hauppage, NY: Barron's Educational.

Straughn, Charles T. & Barbarasue Lovejoy Straughn. *Lovejoy's College Guide.* New York: Macmillan, Updated yearly.

Unger, Harlow G. *But What If I Don't Want to Go to College? A Guide to Success Through Alternative Education.* New York: Facts on File.

Wiener, Solomon & E. P. Steinberg. *Arco Practice for the Armed Services Test, ASVAB.* New York: Macmillan.

Wright, Phillip, Josee Guidry & Judy Blair. *Opportunities for Vocational Study: A Directory of Learning Programs Sponsored by North American Nonprofit Associations.* Toronto: University of Toronto Press.

Yale Daily News Staff. *The Insider's Guide to the Colleges.* New York: St. Martin's Griffin.

Young Person's Occupational Outlook Handbook. Indianapolis: JIST Works.

Part 5

GETTING AND KEEPING YOUR JOB

In this final part of *Creating Your High School Portfolio,* we'll talk about achieving success on the job. You have identified some possible career targets; now you will put together a plan for landing a job in the career area that interests you most.

You also will find some valuable information about keeping your job. People leave jobs for many reasons, and it is best to leave of your own accord. Remember, according to the statistics, you probably will change your job or career several times in your lifetime. That is why it is important to keep your portfolio up-to-date by reviewing it periodically. At some point in your working life you will probably find that your situation, your values, or both have changed significantly since you completed these worksheets. This portfolio was designed with change in mind. The exercises and decision-making process will reflect your needs as they change. This simple process will last your entire working life.

Put Together a Plan

The last three steps in the decision-making model take action on your part. The exercises in this section will help you get started on your job search and make you aware of some essential tools such as resumes and cover letters. There are many resources available to help you find a job, but it all boils down to how much time and energy you are willing to invest in your search. The resource list at the end of Part 5 includes many books and videos that document how to find and keep a job. Consult these resources as necessary (many contain good tips and ideas), but keep in mind that there is no one *best* way to find a job. The best way is the way that works for you.

After you put together your plan of action, share your plan with someone else to hold yourself accountable.

Once you've made your decision, it's time to *do* something about it. The decision becomes your goal, a target for your actions.

Often the difference between dreaming about what you want and making it a reality is putting together a plan of action. Action planning has two major parts: activities and timelines. The next exercise asks you to list your activities (the steps you must take to reach your goal) and to put together a timeline for your goal (when you will accomplish those steps).

After you have completed this exercise, share your plan with a friend. This is a way to make the commitment to carry out the steps and keep yourself on schedule. Find someone who will be supportive of your plans and who can encourage you as you go along. Tell your friend about your deadlines and ask him or her to check with you on your progress. Knowing that someone will ask, "Have you done it yet?" can help motivate you to get things done. After you have filled out your plan, have your friend sign and date it.

Creating Your
**HIGH
SCHOOL
PORTFOLIO**

**GETTING AND
KEEPING
YOUR JOB**

Your Plan of Action

Write your goal on this worksheet. Then list what you must do to get from where you are now to what you must do to accomplish your goal. Work backward from your goal. Give yourself a deadline for each step—this is your timeline. What do you need to do today, tomorrow, next week? Make your deadlines reasonable, but don't allow time for getting sidetracked. After writing down the steps and timelines, sign your plan and date it. Check your plan often as a reminder. Use more paper if you need more space.

My Plan of Action

Write your goal below. What are you going to do and when?

My goal _____

_____

_____

I have worked out a plan for how I will reach my goal. The basic steps, in the order I will take them, are these:

Step _____   When _____

_____   _____

_____   _____

_____   _____

_____   _____

_____   _____

_____   _____

_____   _____

I understand that this is *my plan* and that I have a responsibility to myself to complete it and to review and update it regularly.

Your signature _____   Date _____

I have shared this plan with: _____

Signature _____   Date _____

Act—One Step at a Time

Making a decision and putting together a plan aren't enough to make your plan a reality. You have to take action. The actions you take will depend on the steps you have listed in your plan. For example, the next step in your career plan may be to look for a job. Or you may have decided that you must develop new skills. Perhaps training or education is your next step. Then again, your next step could be something completely different. The key to reaching your goal is to follow your plan, modifying and adding to it as needed. Take the steps one at a time and finish each one according to your plan.

A dream can become a reality—but only if you take action to make it so.

We have included two checklists to help you with the steps for two of the most common goals: job seeking and getting your training and education. The activities are listed for you on the checklists that follow. All you need to do is fill in when you will complete the activity and then check it off when you have finished the task. If your plan takes you directly to job seeking, you'll find worksheets for resumes, cover letters, and interview questions later in this section.

If your goal is taking you in a different direction, such as self-employment or an internship, develop your own checklists, using the checklists that follow as models. Be sure you remember to include all the details in your checklist as you progress with your plan.

Your Job-Seeking Checklist

There are many activities that make up an effective job search. By completing the work in your portfolio thus far, you have already done much to prepare yourself to look for work. The checklist on the following page lists several activities you should complete, many of which you probably already know how to do. Some of these activities, such as preparing a resume and writing cover letters, are topics of the next few worksheets. You may not need to do all the activities in the checklist. For those that will help you, fill in a target date; check off each task as you complete it.

CAUTION

A word about references: Remember that employers prefer to talk to people who know what you can do and who have worked with you. Teachers, former employers, and others who have firsthand knowledge of your skills and strengths can be valuable references. Employers think references from friends and family are not reliable. Be sure to ask people in advance if they would mind being your references, so they're ready when employers call.

GETTING AND KEEPING YOUR JOB

My Job-Seeking Checklist

I will do the following to help me look for a job:

✔ Activity	Target Date	Completed
❏ Ask employers, teachers, and other persons who know about my skills for letters of introduction and/or recommendations and to serve as references for me.		
❏ Talk with friends and family, contacts in business and industry, and others to discuss potential employment contacts (network).		
❏ Update or prepare a resume.		
❏ Prepare a sample cover letter.		
❏ Register at the job service office.		
❏ Plan how to get to employment interviews and job sites.		
❏ Develop a telephone script for making initial inquiries.		
❏ Call or write potential employers.		
❏ Send letters and resumes to potential employers.		
❏ Prepare for interviews by finding out as much as possible about the employer.		
❏ Practice interviewing with friends, family, and other contacts.		
❏ Maintain an active file on employment inquiry contacts.		
❏ Follow up all employment contacts with thank-you notes, telephone contacts, and more information about myself.		

Some important things I need to remember as I look for a job: _____

_____

_____

_____

_____

The Job Application

The job application is an important piece of paperwork that you fill out before an interview or during the hiring process. Often, it gives employers their first look at you. An application reveals three basic—but very strong—characteristics about you.

1. **The ability to prepare and think ahead.** Secretaries and receptionists tell countless stories about unprepared applicants who ask for pens, pencils, and telephone books. They often hand out several applications because job seekers make mistakes filling them out. Do receptionists tell interviewers about these people? You bet they do! Be prepared! Bring these items with you:

   ▼ An information worksheet ("My Job Application Fact Sheet").

   ▼ Pens and pencils (It helps to have an erasable fine-tip pen.).

   ▼ A resume to submit with the application or to leave with the employer.

2. **The ability to follow instructions and to use accurate information.** Every job requires some ability to read, understand, and follow written instructions, rules, or procedures. It is critical to fill out the information correctly. Here are some basic tips:

   ▼ Read the entire application before you start to fill it out. Make sure you understand the instructions in each section.

   ▼ Follow the instructions exactly. If the application says "print," then print your information. Leave those sections blank that say, "For employer's use only" or "Do not write below this line." Some applications ask you to list your most recent job first; others want the list in the reverse order. Read carefully.

   ▼ Be honest. If you are hired for the job and your employer discovers that you have intentionally lied on the application, you may be fired.

3. **The ability to complete a document neatly and to follow through on a task.** Crossed-out or poorly erased information gives a negative impression that reflects on the quality of your work. If you leave sections or lines blank or write in "See above" or "See resume," the employer may think you won't follow through on the details of a job. Of course, some questions don't apply to every applicant. A proper response to this is to put "N/A" (nonapplicable) in the space.

Your Job Application Fact Sheet

You can use the fact sheet that follows to organize the information you will need as you fill out applications. Complete the form and take it with you as a reference when you fill out a job application or have an interview. You gathered much of this information in Part 1.

When filling out applications, keep the following in mind:

▼ Follow instructions.

▼ Be neat.

▼ Be accurate.

▼ Be honest.

▼ Complete the entire form.

▼ Write clearly.

▼ Get permission before using a reference.

▼ Sign the application if requested.

My Job Application Fact Sheet

Identification

Your name: First _____ Middle _____ Last _____

Your current address: Street _____

City _____ State _____ Zip code _____

Your current phone number or a number where a message can be left _____

E-mail address _____

Social Security number _____

Driver's license number _____

Name and number of a person to contact in an emergency _____

Job desired/Job requirements_____

_____

_____

Name of position for which you are applying _____

Date you are available to begin work _____

Salary or pay rate expected _____

Previous Employment

(Use information from "My Work Experience" worksheet in Part 2.)

Job title _____

Employer _____

Street address _____

City/State/Zip _____

Phone/Fax _____

Dates _____ Reason for leaving _____

Special skills demonstrated _____

_____

_____

Job title _____

Employer _____

Street address _____

City/State/Zip _____

Phone/Fax _____

Dates _____ Reason for leaving _____

Special skills demonstrated _____

_____

_____

Job title _____

Employer _____

Street address _____

City/State/Zip _____

Phone/Fax _____

Dates _____ Reason for leaving _____

Special skills demonstrated _____

_____

_____

Copyright © 1998 • JIST Works, Inc. • Indianapolis, IN 46216 • 1-800-648-JIST

125

GETTING AND KEEPING YOUR JOB

Formal Education

School most recently attended _____

Address _____

Dates attended _____   Degree earned _____

Activities (honors, clubs, sports) _____

_____

School _____

Address _____

Dates attended _____   Degree earned _____

Activities (honors, clubs, sports) _____

_____

References

Name _____

Address _____

Phone _____

Relationship (employer, teacher, coworker, clergy) _____

Name _____

Address _____

Phone _____

Relationship (employer, teacher, coworker, clergy) _____

Name _____

Address _____

Phone _____

Relationship (employer, teacher, coworker, clergy) _____

The Resume

In completing Parts 1 and 2, you have done much of the work needed to put together or update your resume. These days, employers want more than a list of job duties or where you worked and when. They are interested in how well you did your job, what skills and experience you have to offer, your strengths, and what you accomplished. Go back to Parts 1 and 2 and extract the information from the worksheets listed below to include in your resume.

▼ My Personality Style

▼ My Work Experience

▼ My Home/Leisure/Community Activities

▼ Things I've Done That Made Me Proud

▼ What I Can Do

▼ My Personal Qualities

Also look through the other documents you have filed in your portfolio. Review your educational records, training certificates, and letters of recommendation or performance evaluations for information you may want to include in your resume (or in a cover letter).

The goal of writing a resume is to include just enough information to get an interview with the employer. Save the detailed information for the interview. Think of a resume as an advertisement to get an interview. Advertisements are perfect (no errors or spelling mistakes), easy to read, and appealing to the eye. The same should be true for your resume.

Your resume should:

▼ Be free of spelling, punctuation, grammar, or keyboard errors

▼ Be short, concise, and specific

▼ Emphasize accomplishments and benefits to the employer

▼ Highlight skills and strengths related to the target job

▼ Appeal to the eye and be printed on quality paper

There are many ways to put a resume together. But there are two important points to remember:

1. **The most effective resume is one that focuses on the requirements of the job.** This means you may need to customize your resume to match the requirements of a specific job. You may need two or three versions of your resume if you are applying for different kinds of jobs. Although you will use the same basic information in each one, you will arrange and emphasize your skills, abilities, strengths, and background information differently to match the requirements of each job. This may sound like a difficult task, but if you have access to a computer and can use a word-processing program to do your resume, you'll be amazed at how easy it is to tailor your resume to each job. If you don't have access to a computer, perhaps you can have your resume done by someone who has one and wouldn't mind making your alterations for you. Most people who provide resume-typing services use word-processing programs.

   A second-best alternative is to use customized cover letters to list the most important information about you that matches each job's requirements. (We'll talk about cover letters next.)

2. **Your most important assets—the information you want to be *sure* the employer reads—should be highlighted in the "prime space" area of your resume.** The first thing an employer reads is the top half of the first page of your resume. This area—the prime space—should contain the most important information you want the employer to know about you. As you write your resume, ask yourself this question: What is the most important information I want this employer to know about me when considering me for this job? Is it:

   ▼ My current or most recent job?   ▼ My recent training?

   ▼ A summary of my experience?   ▼ My education?

   ▼ A list of my skills and strengths?   ▼ My achievements?

Choose what is most important for the particular job and place this information in the prime space.

Your name, address, and phone number are usually centered at the top of the page. Bold lettering or dividing the sections of your resume with lines makes it easier to read. You also may want to use bold type or underline the highlights, such as the companies for which you have worked and your employment dates. That way, a prospective employer can scan the page and immediately see this information.

Keep copies of your resumes (and cover letters) in your portfolio so you can refer to them in the future. It is much easier to update or rearrange an old resume than to start from the beginning each time you need one.

GETTING AND KEEPING YOUR JOB

Your Resume Worksheet

Use this simple outline as a guideline to assemble all the essential elements your resume should list. After you have the information together, play around with the format until you have a design that is both functional and agreeable to the eye. If you need more help on constructing your resume, consult the list of resources at the end of this section.

My Resume Worksheet

_____
Name

_____
Address

_____
Telephone

_____

Objective _____
(What kind of position you want)

Education or Training   PRIME SPACE
(Recent and focused on job target) _____
_____
_____
(Refer to items you filed from the list in "What Can You Offer?") _____
_____
_____

Current or Last Job
(Use information from the "My Work Experience" section.) _____
_____
_____

List of Skills
(Refer to the "What I Can Do" worksheet.) _____
_____
_____

GETTING AND KEEPING YOUR JOB

PRIME SPACE

List of Achievements
(Refer to "Things I've Done That Made Me Proud.") _____
_____
_____
_____

Summary of Experience
(Review Parts 1 and 2.) _____
_____
_____
_____
_____

Highlights of Qualifications
(Outline most important parts of "What I Can Do.") _____
_____
_____
_____

Employment History
(Use information from "My Work Experience.") _____
_____
_____
_____
_____
_____
_____
_____
_____
_____
_____
_____
_____
_____

Education and Training
(If not listed above, refer to "What Can You Offer?") _____
_____

The Cover Letter

In the past, most cover letters merely told the employer where the applicant heard about the job and stated that a resume was attached. Today's cover letter is used for a variety of purposes:

> You probably will spend a lot of time and effort to ensure that your resume is "perfect" —and rightly so. But if you send it with a cover letter that contains even one conspicuous error, all of your effort will be wasted.

- ▼ Links the name of a person (a reference) known to both the applicant and the employer

- ▼ Indicates the applicant's interest in the job

- ▼ Indicates the job seeker's knowledge of the organization

- ▼ Lists additional information not included in the resume

- ▼ Emphasizes skills, background, and strengths that match the job requirements

- ▼ Explains special circumstances

- ▼ Asks for an interview or indicates the job seeker's follow-up plan

To be effective, your cover letter:

- ▼ Must be free of spelling, punctuation, grammar, and keyboard errors

- ▼ Must use standard business letter format and be printed on quality paper

- ▼ Should be addressed to an individual by name and title, if possible

Keep your cover letter short (one page) and make sure it is easy to read. Avoid long paragraphs. Use short lists. If you are unsure about proper spelling and grammar, use a good dictionary and ask someone who has good writing skills to proofread it for you.

Your Cover Letter Outline

Your cover letter is the perfect place to deliver customized communication to your prospective employer. It introduces your resume to the employer and can draw attention to something you want to highlight. Use your network to get names and then address your cover letter to a specific person in each organization. If you are persistent and creative, you will find the contact you need.

My Cover Letter Outline

Fill in the spaces below and use the information to compose your own personalized cover letter.

Date _____

Name of company contact person _____
Street address of company _____
City, state, and zip code _____

Dear Mr./Ms. _____ :

What I know about the company or industry I am applying to (might include the name of a referral): _____
_____
_____

What I know about the position (might include how you, if hired, can perform well in that position): _____
_____
_____

Skills, abilities, and strengths I can bring to the position (how your knowledge and skills can assist the company in meeting its goals): _____
_____

Recap, follow-up plan, request for an interview, or thank you: _____
_____

Sincerely,
(Write your signature here) _____
Type your name as it is written in signature _____

Making Contact

In the "Networking" section of your portfolio, you listed people you could contact for career information. You can use those same individuals for your job-seeking network. They can now provide you with employer contacts and information about job openings. The goal is to expand your network so that you have many sources of information. One great inexpensive way of expanding your network is to let your fingers do the walking.

People generally want to help other people, but only if you make it easy for them to help you. Do your homework first and remember that by accepting help, you are obligated to give help to others in your network when the time comes.

Many job seekers say that making telephone inquiries is a difficult thing to do. If picking up the phone to make a call to a potential employer is hard for you, having a telephone script can help. A script should include the following information:

▼ A greeting

▼ Your name

▼ The name of your contact who suggested the call

▼ The purpose of your call

▼ Two or three things about you that will interest the employer

▼ A request for a face-to-face meeting

If you still find yourself uncomfortable talking to a stranger about job openings over the telephone, start with someone you know. Then call the people whose names they gave you, or others in your network whom you don't personally know.

Sometimes an employer insists on interviewing you over the phone. (Remember, this is a good thing.) Keep your resume at hand to help you remember what you want to say about yourself. If you are interviewed over the telephone after making a cold call, send your resume along with a thank-you letter to the employer as a follow-up.

Your Telephone Script

This worksheet will help you develop a phone script. When you have completed this exercise, practice saying your script aloud in a mirror or into a tape recorder. Keep refining your script until you are comfortable speaking and the words feel natural. Be sure your script is not too long. You don't want to sound like a telemarketer, but you do want to sell yourself. That means you need to get across all your vital information in the first 30 seconds or so. (It's not a bad idea to time yourself when you practice saying your script aloud.) Ask a friend or your counselor to listen to your script and ask for feedback. File a copy of your final phone script in your portfolio.

My Telephone Script

Fill in the information below to help you organize your thoughts and create your personalized phone script.

Good morning, my name is _____ :

I'm calling at the suggestion of _____ , a business acquaintance of yours. He/she said you might know of an opening in your organization (or other organization) that could use a person of my abilities.

I have over _____ years of experience in (list your skills, abilities, and strengths that you can contribute to this organization and, if possible, indicate how well you performed your tasks and responsibilities). _____

_____

_____

_____

_____

When would be a good time to come in for an interview? (Do not ask if you **may** come in for an interview. Make it hard for the employer to turn you down. After all, your goal is to get an interview.)

Preparing for Interviews

The more you prepare for an interview, the better you will do. The two key steps to preparing for interviews are finding out about the employer and practicing.

Employers like applicants who take the time to get information about the job and the company. Applicants who have done their homework give the impression that they have carefully selected a potential job and company rather than applied for just any job opening. Background information will help you decide whether the job and organization fit you. This information is available through the following resources:

- ▼ People in your network, or those who work for the company
- ▼ Job postings
- ▼ Company brochures
- ▼ Company Web sites
- ▼ Reference material in the library, particularly periodicals
- ▼ Public or private placement services

You may have skills and abilities an employer is looking for, but if you can't communicate what you can do, you may not get the job. Here's where practice helps. Many employers ask standard questions in an interview. The questions generally fall into a few categories, such as work history and experience, strengths and weaknesses, goals, education or training history, and how well you fit the job and the organization.

Many job-seeking books or government pamphlets contain lists of frequently asked interview questions. Use these lists and practice answering the questions. Spend more time on the ones that seem hard to answer. Sometimes high schools, colleges or universities, or job training agencies have workshops on interviewing.

Some more tips to remember include these:

- ▼ Go into the interview with a positive attitude.
- ▼ Give complete but concise answers to the questions.
- ▼ Do not make negative comments about previous employers or coworkers. It's impossible to stress how important this is. You *must* find a way to be positive about your previous experiences and forget about the negatives when you are interviewing, even if you have deep-seated resentment against an employer who fired you or treated you badly.
- ▼ Keep your remarks targeted to the job. Sometimes even an interviewer gets off the subject, but try to remain focused on the matter at hand.
- ▼ Leave any personal concerns at home. Personal baggage can only hinder your chances.

GETTING AND KEEPING YOUR JOB

Questions to Prepare for Your Interview

Below are some questions employers frequently ask. If you have completed Parts 1 and 2, you should be able to answer all of them. Write your answers on the worksheet, or record them on an audio or video tape, and practice answering them in front of a mirror or with a friend who will give you good advice. Another method is to find someone who has hiring and interviewing experience to coach you and tell you what you're doing right and where you could improve.

Questions to Prepare for My Interview

1. Tell me something about yourself. _____

_____

2. Why are you interested in this job? _____

_____

3. What kind of work have you been doing? _____

_____

4. What would previous employers say about you? _____

_____

5. What are your strongest skills? How have you used them? _____

_____

6. What are two areas that you need to work on? _____

_____

7. What would you like to improve about yourself? Why? How? _____

_____

_____

8. What have you learned from previous jobs? _____

_____

9. What is your most significant work experience?_____

_____

10. Why should I hire you for this job? _____

_____

Following Up

Many employers say that the way people search for work tells them what kind of employees they will be. Employers would rather give the job to someone who really wants it than to someone who doesn't seem to care. Following up after making a contact or having an interview shows the employer how eager you are to get the job.

Consider the following:

▼ You may be the only applicant who takes the time to write a follow-up note or make a phone call.

▼ Your follow-up is an opportunity to tell the employer something you may have forgotten to mention in the interview.

▼ The employer may have several job openings. If you are not right for one, you might be right for another. Your follow-up gives the employer a reason to take another look at you.

For Additional Help

If you need more training in job-seeking techniques, look for books or videos in the library or at a nearby bookstore. Make sure that the materials you use are the most up-to-date you can find. Check the copyright dates.

Job-seeking resources can provide materials such as these:

▼ Sample resumes for a variety of jobs

▼ Various resume formats to choose from

▼ Resume writing do's and don'ts

▼ Sample cover letters

▼ Information about networking and interviewing

Remember, high schools, vocational schools, colleges and universities, community agencies, or government services may have job-search programs in your area. Check your local library or newspaper for schedule information.

Your First Week at Work—Keeping Your New Job After You Get It

The first few days on the job are referred to as a honeymoon. This is because the employer is pleased to have you working and does not yet expect you to know everything about the workplace and the tasks of the job.

This is the time for you to demonstrate and begin to document your success on the job, as well as to show your interest in how the organization works and to get to know your supervisor and coworkers. It is important to use the first few days to learn as much as you can about the job and your new working environment. Don't be afraid to ask questions. One of the biggest mistakes new workers make is not asking enough questions at the beginning—and asking too many later on.

The survival of an organization depends on the quality of its workforce at all levels. Employers agree that the ability of an employee to keep a job depends on the worker's success in these four basic areas:

1. **Dependability and reliability.** Frequent absences or absences without good reasons are cause for dismissal. Employers also rely on workers to follow through on tasks given them.

2. **Punctuality.** Employers expect their employees to report for work on time. Workers who are late at the start of work, for meetings, or returning from lunch or breaks delay the work of others and cause problems for coworkers, supervisors, and customers.

3. **Quality of work.** Employers depend on workers to produce a quality product or service. Not only is quality important in competing with other organizations that provide the same product or service, it is a key to company and job survival.

4. **Quantity of work.** Productivity is also one of the most important elements in keeping a job. A successful worker is one who produces more than enough goods or services to justify his or her wage, and who keeps costs down to help the organization make a profit.

If you keep these four attributes in mind as you begin a new job and throughout your career, you will become a quality employee.

Creating Your
HIGH SCHOOL PORTFOLIO

GETTING AND KEEPING YOUR JOB

Your First Week Checklist

This checklist has some areas you should explore in your first week at a new job. Most of the information here will be provided by your supervisor. Remember—*ask, don't guess!*

My First Week Checklist

Check the statement if you have learned about it at your new job.

✔ **Schedule**	✔ **Organizational Structure**
❑ Working hours	❑ Who supervises whom
❑ Reporting-to-work time	❑ Name of supervisor's boss
❑ Lunch hours	❑ Name of supervisor
❑ Break times	❑ Names of coworkers

✔ Pay

❑ Payday

❑ Method of payment

❑ Accessing benefits

❑ If applicable: shift differential or overtime pay

✔ Job

❑ Job description

❑ Detailed discussion of tasks and responsibilities

❑ Work area

❑ How your job fits into overall operation

❑ Whom to ask when you have questions

❑ How you will be evaluated, when, and by whom

✔ Policies

❑ Absences: whom to notify, by whom, number to call

❑ Lateness

❑ Security/Confidentiality

❑ Smoking

❑ Parking

Growing on the Job

The workplace of the future demands constant learning and growing. Employers expect more from their workers today than they did in the past. Global competition, changing technology, and the need for a highly skilled workforce combine to make employers very careful about whom they hire, whom they keep, and whom they promote. In addition to the four basic elements listed in the previous section, employers agree that in order to grow on the job, employees should be able to do these things:

1. **Know how to learn.** Realize the importance of career-long learning and take advantage of on-the-job or after-work training.

2. **Read, write, and do computation.** Improve these skills, which are critical to learning new job functions.

3. **Listen and communicate.** Understand instructions and problems and communicate effectively with coworkers, supervisors, and customers.

4. **Be adaptable.** Adapt to changes in technology and on the job, solve problems in a creative way, and try new ideas and methods.

5. **Work as part of a team.** Work effectively with others; lead when necessary; and work with others from different gender, age, racial, or cultural backgrounds.

6. **Provide outstanding customer service.** Look for ways to improve service to internal and external customers.

7. **Manage yourself.** Be a self-starter, be honest and ethical, take responsibility for your actions, and look for ways to develop and improve skills and traits important to the job and the organization.

You will be a more valuable asset to your organization and happier with yourself if you keep learning new skills, taking more responsibilities, and identifying and pursuing new directions for your personal and professional growth.

Refer to the "What I Can Do" section of your portfolio, where you listed documentation or demonstration notes about similar skills. As you read through those qualities essential to job success, ask yourself these questions:

▼ Do I do these effectively? Somewhat effectively? Not effectively?

▼ Which ones could I work on to improve my success on the job?

▼ How could I work on them?

Use the same planning and decision-making process outlined in your portfolio to develop a plan for keeping your job and growing on the job.

Your Areas for Growth

Following through with the statements on this worksheet will keep you current with the changing workplace and make you a more valuable and satisfied worker. Make a commitment to yourself to take the actions listed below. You don't have to do everything on the checklist at once, but refer to it regularly to see if there are areas in which you can grow.

My Areas for Growth

Read each statement below. Place a **P** for those actions you have done in the past, a **C** for those actions you are doing currently, and an **F** for those actions you commit to do in the future.

_____ I honestly evaluate the quality and quantity of my work, my follow-through, my punctuality, and my reliability.

_____ I show a positive attitude on the job.

_____ I get feedback from my supervisor on a regular basis on my specific areas of strength and weakness.

_____ I get feedback from customers and coworkers on my performance.

_____ I ask my supervisor to help me set performance goals. If this is not possible, I set them on my own.

_____ When evaluated, I try to identify areas and opportunities for growth.

_____ I let my supervisor know what I have accomplished.

_____ I take advantage of company-offered training.

_____ I get training, if available, on my own time.

_____ I get involved with company-paid classes or tuition reimbursement programs.

_____ I volunteer for new assignments, especially if they involve learning new skills.

_____ I volunteer for more responsibility.

Other areas of growth are these: _____

_____

Evaluate Your Progress—and Modify

If you have worked through *Creating Your High School Portfolio* from the beginning, you have completed these seven of the eight steps in the "Model for Career Decision Making."

> *"Make no little plans; they have no magic to stir men's blood and probably themselves will not be realized. Make big plans; aim high in hope and work..."*
>
> —David H. Burnham

1. Decide to decide.

2. Gather information about yourself.

3. Explore what's out there.

4. Generate options and consequences.

5. Make a decision.

6. Put together a plan.

7. Act.

The last step is to evaluate the progress you have made toward your goal. To check on how you are doing, answer the questions in the "My Plan Is in Progress" worksheet on the next page. You may find that you are on track. You may discover something about your plan, your situation, or yourself that has changed your goal or changed the steps necessary to reach that goal. Remember, the plan and the decision are yours alone. You can evaluate and change either one at any point.

TIP

"The race is over, but the work never is done while the power to work remains."

—Justice Oliver Wendell Holmes

GETTING AND
KEEPING
YOUR JOB

Your Plan Is in Progress

Look again at the plan you wrote out at the beginning of this section. Do you need to review one of the steps to make your plan more workable? Did you skip a step or two that might provide information for making a better plan? Don't lose sight of your goals. Make your decisions work for you, even if it means starting over using new information.

My Plan Is in Progress

Answer the questions to evaluate the progress of your plan.

What new pieces of information could I add to my decision-making worksheet? _____

_____

_____

How will the new information change my decision? _____

_____

_____

Have I reached my goal? If not, what is keeping me from progressing? _____

_____

_____

If I have reached my goal, what is my new goal? (Remember to start the decision-making

process again.) _____

_____

_____

I will evaluate my progress again in (days, weeks, months, year). _____

_____

_____

Getting and Keeping Your Job Checklist

This final checklist will help you see if you have developed skills in career planning and job seeking.

Getting and Keeping My Job Checklist

Put a check mark next to those items you have learned to do.

_____   I can identify the components of a career plan.

_____   I can develop an individual career plan or update information from earlier plans.

_____   I can identify activities for job seeking.

_____   I can identify activities to get further education or training.

_____   I can evaluate my progress toward my career goal.

Useful ideas for me to remember in career planning: _____

_____

_____

_____

Helpful advice and counseling I have received while exploring and planning my

career: _____

_____

_____

_____

GETTING AND KEEPING YOUR JOB

Your Journal Entry

Now that you have completed the exercises for your portfolio and evaluated your progress as you work toward your goal, do you feel you have made a satisfying decision? Why or why not? If the decision feels unsatisfying, will you still follow through with your plan? Have you ever made an unsatisfying decision for a "satisfying" reason?

My Journal Entry

Think of a time when you were faced with a difficult decision. Given what you have now learned about yourself, would you have made the same decision? Why? What would you have done differently? Would the outcome have been the same? Do you think it is possible to make satisfying decisions all the time?

_____

_____

_____

_____

_____

_____

_____

_____

_____

_____

_____

_____

_____

_____

_____

_____

Career Planning Is Ongoing

Because of the work you've done to complete your portfolio, you have learned a way to make career decisions that you can use over and over when considering the following situations:

▼ A job change

▼ A promotion or other career move

▼ New training

▼ More education

▼ Activities outside of work

Your portfolio is an ongoing product of your work. Revise all of its parts as you complete your educational goals and have new career experiences. It is important and useful to future decisions that you add new personal details, new career information, and new decisions and goals. The next time, you won't need to start from the beginning. You can review the information already in your portfolio. Then it will be easy to explore new opportunities. You can move quickly toward new decisions and plans.

Congratulations for investing in your future!

List of Resources

Associations

Entrepreneurship Institute, 3592 Corporate Drive, Suite 101, Columbus, OH 43231. 614/895-1153. http://www.tei.net

Professional Association of Resume Writers, 3637 Fourth Street North, Suite 330, St. Petersburg, FL, 33704. 813/821-2274. http://www.parw.com

U.S. Small Business Administration, Imperial Building, 1441 L Street, NW, Washington, DC 20415. 202/653-7561. http://www.sba.gov

Books

Beatty, Richard H. *The Perfect Cover Letter,* 2nd Edition. New York: Wiley.

Bolles, Richard Nelson. *What Color Is Your Parachute?* Berkeley, CA: Ten Speed Press.

America's Top 300 Jobs: A Complete Career Handbook. Indianapolis: JIST Works.

Farr, J. Michael. *America's Top Resumes for America's Top Jobs.*™ Indianapolis: JIST Works.

Farr, J. Michael. *The Quick Interview & Salary Negotiation Book: Dramatically Improve Your Interviewing Skills in Just a Few Hours!* Indianapolis: JIST Works.

Farr, J. Michael. *The Quick Resume & Cover Letter Book: Write and Use an Effective Resume in Only One Day.* Indianapolis: JIST Works.

Farr, J. Michael. *The Very Quick Job Search,* 2nd Edition: *Get a Better Job in Half the Time!* Indianapolis: JIST Works.

Jandt, Fred E., and Mary B. Nemnich. *Using the Internet and the World Wide Web in Your Job Search.* Indianapolis: JIST Works.

Lauber, Daniel. *Professional Job Finder.* River Forest, IL: Planning Communications.

LeCompte, Michelle. *Job Hunter's Sourcebook: Where to Find Employment Leads and Other Job Search Resources,* 3ʳᵈ Edition. Detroit: Gale Research.

Ludden, LaVerne L. *Job Savvy,* 2ⁿᵈ Edition: *How to Be a Success at Work.* Indianapolis: JIST Works.

Marcus, John J. *The Complete Job Interview Handbook,* 3ʳᵈ Edition. New York: Harper Perennial.

Noble, David F. *Gallery of Best Resumes.* Indianapolis: JIST Works.

Noble, David F. *Gallery of Best Resumes for Two-Year Degree Graduates.* Indianapolis: JIST Works.

Peterson's Hidden Job Market. Princeton, NJ: Peterson's Guides, Updated yearly.

Riley, Margaret, et al. *The Guide to Internet Job Searching.* Lincolnwood, IL: VGM Career Horizons.

Sabin, William A. *The Gregg Reference Manual,* 8ᵗʰ Edition. Mission Hills, CA: Glencoe/McGraw-Hill.

Swanson, David. *The Resume Solution,* Revised Edition. Indianapolis: JIST Works.

Troutman, Kathryn K. *The Federal Resume Guidebook.* Indianapolis: JIST Works.

Software

Adams Electronic Job Search Almanac. Holbrook, MA: Bob Adams.

Discovering Careers and Jobs Plus. Detroit: Gale Research.

PFS Resume & Job Search Pro. Cambridge, MA: Softkey International.

WinWay Resume, Sacramento, CA: WinWay Corporation.

Videos

Barton, Jim. *Jim Barton's the Job Interview and You*. Montvale, NJ : Career PathProds.

Farr, J. Michael. *The Very Quick Job Search Video,* 2nd Edition. Indianapolis: JIST Works.

How to Find & Keep a Job Video Series. Indianapolis: JIST Works.

Job Survival Skills, Revised. Indianapolis: JIST Works.

Resume Remedy. Indianapolis: JIST Works.

Transitions: Choices for Mid-Career Changers. Indianapolis: Park Avenue Productions.

Best Jobs for the 21ˢᵗ Century

By J. Michael Farr and Laverne L. Ludden, Ed.D.

This data-packed reference is ideal for students, teachers, working people, and anyone interested in career planning and job advancement:

- Contains over 50 lists of jobs with the best pay, fastest growth, and most openings by numerous categories

- Describes 686 jobs with fast growth or high pay

- Based on expert analysis of labor and economic trends

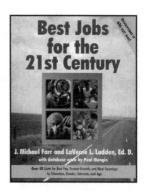

ISBN 1-56370-486-2 $19.95
Order Code LP-J4862

Occupational Outlook Handbook

By the U.S. Department of Labor

The *Occupational Outlook Handbook* is the most widely used career exploration resource. This is a quality reprint of the government's *OOH,* only at a less-expensive price. It describes 250 jobs–jobs held by almost 90 percent of the U.S. workforce–making it ideal for students, counselors, teachers, librarians, and job seekers.

- Well-written narrative with many charts and photos

- Job descriptions cover the nature of the work, working conditions, training, job outlook, and earnings

- New edition every two years

ISBN 1-56370-676-8 $18.95
Softcover   Order Code LP-J6768

ISBN 1-56370-677-6 $22.95
Hardcover   Order Code LP-J6776

The College Majors Handbook

The Actual Jobs, Earnings, and Trends for Graduates of 60 College Majors

By Neeta P. Fogg, Paul E. Harrington, and Thomas F. Harrington

Are your students faced with the college decision? Here's a book detailing what actually happened to more than 150,000 undergraduates from 60 college majors.

ISBN 1-56370-518-4 $24.95
Order Code LP-J5184

- The only college planning guide with the perspective of what actually happened to college undergraduates

- Identifies jobs in which undergraduates from 60 college majors are employed and their earnings on those jobs

Creating Your High School Resume

A Step-by-Step Guide to Preparing an Effective Resume for College and Career

By Kathryn Kraemer Troutman

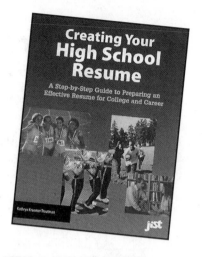

A great workbook that shows students how to turn classes, activities, and accomplishments into resumes that get results

Creating Your High School Resume takes students step-by-step through the resume-writing process. Whether college-bound or going straight to work, students learn to articulate and document their skills, interests, and experiences into their first resume.

ISBN 1-56370-508-7
Order Code LP-J5087
Paperbound
144 pages
Reasonably priced at $7.95

- Straightforward questions help students build resumes section-by-section—from start to finish.

- Inspiring case studies of real students reveal the rationale behind their resumes.

- Dozens of high-interest examples show how to focus, organize, write, and format resumes.

- Clear narration explains how resumes can help students find jobs and apply for internships and college.

- Friendly tips remind students about the importance of correct grammar, proofreading, and consistency.

Creating Your High School Resume addresses today's technology and shows students how to do the following:

- Create the best format for their resumes with word processors or desktop publishing programs.

- Use the Web and e-mail effectively for research and contacts.

- Manage electronic resume files efficiently.

- Design a scannable resume that will make the cut at big companies.

The workbook gives your students helpful job-search information on how to

- Find a mentor, build a network, and get informational interviews.

- Write strong cover letters, thank-you letters, and reference lists.

- Find openings, approach employers, and do well in interviews.

Table of Contents

The O*NET Dictionary of Occupational Titles

Based on data from the U.S. Department of Labor

Compiled by J. Michael Farr and LaVerne L. Ludden, Ed.D., with database work by Paul Mangin

JIST is the first publisher to use the U.S. Department of Labor's new O*NET data, which was developed to replace the 1991 edition of the *Dictionary of Occupational Titles*. The O*NET presents a major change in occupational information systems, and this new reference includes

- Descriptions of all major jobs–more than 1,100–in the new O*NET database

- User-friendly introduction to the O*NET system

ISBN 1-56370-510-9 $39.95
Softcover   Order Code LP-J5109

ISBN 1-56370-509-5 $49.95
Hardcover   Order Code LP-J5095

Career Guide to Industries

A Companion Reference to the Occupational Outlook Handbook

By the U.S. Department of Labor

This information-packed review of 40 top industries discusses employment trends, earnings, types of jobs available, working conditions, training required, and more. Helpful for career-minded people interested in certain industries.

- Discusses careers from an industry perspective

- Companion book to the *Occupational Outlook Handbook*, which discusses jobs from an occupational perspective

- Extremely valuable to those making career-related decisions of all kinds

ISBN 1-56370-804-3 $16.95
Order Code LP-8043

Enhanced Occupational Outlook Handbook, Third Edition

Based on data from the U.S. Department of Labor

Compiled by J. Michael Farr and LaVerne L. Ludden, Ed.D., with database work by Paul Mangin

This award-winning book combines the best features of America's three most authoritative occupational references–the *Occupational Outlook Handbook*, the *Dictionary of Occupational Titles*, and now, the O*NET (the Department of Labor's Occupational Information Network).

- Huge 864-page reference with over 3,600 job descriptions

- Helps readers identify major jobs of interest and then obtain information on these jobs and the many more specialized jobs related to them

ISBN 1-56370-801-9 $37.95
Softcover   Order Code LP-J8019

ISBN 1-56370-802-7 $44.95
Hardcover   Order Code LP-J8027

JIST Order and Catalog Request Form

Purchase Order #: _____ (Required by some organizations)

Billing Information

Organization Name: _____

Accounting Contact: _____

Street Address: _____

_____

_____

City, State, Zip: _____

Phone Number: (   ) _____

Shipping Information with Street Address (If Different from Above)

Organization Name: _____

Contact: _____

Street Address: (We *cannot* ship to P.O. boxes) _____

_____

_____

City, State, Zip: _____

Phone Number: (   ) _____

> **Please copy this form if you need more lines for your order.**

> **Phone: 1-800-648-JIST**
> **Fax: 1-800-JIST-FAX**
> **World Wide Web Address:**
> **http://www.jist.com**

Credit Card Purchases: VISA____ MC____ AMEX____

Card Number: _____

Exp. Date: _____

Name As on Card: _____

Signature: _____

Quantity	Order Code	Product Title	Unit Price	Total
	———	**Free JIST Catalog**	Free	———

JIST Publishing
8902 Otis Avenue
Indianapolis, IN 46216

Shipping / Handling / Insurance Fees

In the continental U.S. add 7% of subtotal:
- Minimum amount charged = $4.00
- Maximum amount charged = $100.00
- FREE shipping and handling on any prepaid orders over $40.00

Above pricing is for regular ground shipment only. For rush or special delivery, call JIST Customer Service at 1-800-648-JIST for the correct shipping fee.

Outside the continental U.S. call JIST Customer Service at 1-800-648-JIST for an estimate of these fees.

Payment in U.S. funds only!

Subtotal	
+5% Sales Tax Indiana Residents	
+Shipping / Handling / Ins. (See left)	
TOTAL	

JIST thanks you for your order!